Passport's

JAPAN

FROM
THOMAS
COOK

PASSPORT BOOKS
a division of *NTC Publishing Group*
Lincolnwood, Illinois USA

Published by Passport Books,
a division of NTC Publishing Group,
4255 W. Touhy Avenue,
Lincolnwood (Chicago), Illinois
60646–1975 U.S.A.

Written by Lauren Deakin

Original photography by Jim Holmes

Edited, designed and produced by AA Publishing.
© The Automobile Association 1996.
Maps © The Automobile Association 1996.

Library of Congress Catalog Card Number:
95-73298

ISBN 0-8442-4828-2

The contents of this publication are believed correct at the time of
printing. Nevertheless, the publishers cannot accept responsibility for
any errors or omissions, or for changes in the details given in this guide,
or for the consequences of any reliance on the information provided by
the same. Assessments of attractions, hotels, restaurants, and so forth
are based upon the author's own experience, and therefore descriptions
given in this guide necessarily contain an element of subjective opinion
which may not reflect the publisher's opinion or dictate a reader's own
experiences on another occasion.
We have tried to ensure accuracy in this guide, but things do
change and we would be grateful if readers would advise us of any
inaccuracies they may encounter.

Published by Passport Books in conjunction with AA Publishing and the
Thomas Cook Group Ltd.

Color separation: BTB Colour Reproduction, Whitchurch, Hampshire,
England.

Printed by Edicoes ASA, Oporto, Portugal.

Contents

About this Book

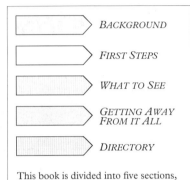

BACKGROUND

FIRST STEPS

WHAT TO SEE

GETTING AWAY FROM IT ALL

DIRECTORY

This book is divided into five sections, identified by the above colour coding.

Background gives an introduction to the country – its history, geography, politics, culture.

First Steps offers practical advice on arriving and getting around.

What to See is an alphabetical listing of places to visit, interspersed with walks and tours.

Getting Away From it All highlights places off the beaten track where it's possible to relax and enjoy peace and quiet.

Finally, the **Directory** provides practical information – from shopping and entertainment to children and sport, including a section on business matters. Special highly illustrated features on specific aspects of the country appear throughout the book.

Shibuya crossing: the bustling heart of fashionable Tokyo

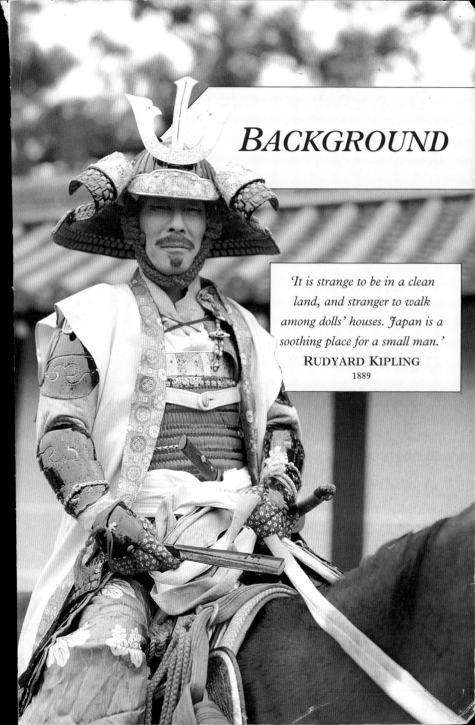

BACKGROUND

'It is strange to be in a clean
land, and stranger to walk
among dolls' houses. Japan is a
soothing place for a small man.'
RUDYARD KIPLING
1889

Introduction

*J*apan is a beguiling mix of opposites – old and new, east and west; the most modern of countries, it retains at the same time its ancient traditions and an awareness of thousands of years of history.

COUNTRY LOCATOR

Japan does not give up its secrets easily. It is worth taking time to explore, and travelling is a joy. There are futuristic trains, fast and punctual, and excellent roads leading to obscure corners of the country. There is almost no random crime, and despite its reputation for outrageous expense, you can find cheap inns and restaurants nearly everywhere you go. This is the country of crazy modern buildings, and of ancient castles and palaces; of energy, wealth and novelty, and of serene Buddhist temples. It is a country like nowhere else on earth.

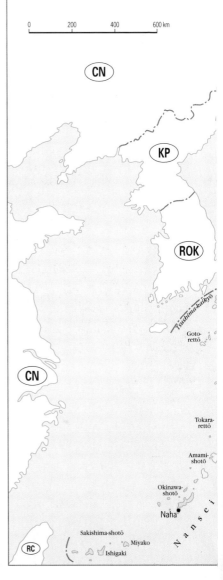

JAPAN

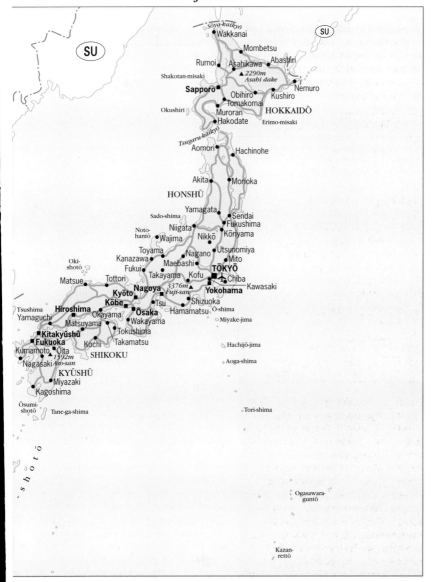

Sōya-kaikyō
Wakkanai
SU
Mombetsu
Rumoi
Asahikawa
Abashiri
Shakotan-misaki
▲ 2290m
Asahi dake
Sapporo
Nemuro
Obihiro
Kushiro
Tomakomai
HOKKAIDŌ
Okushiri
Muroran
Hakodate
Erimo-misaki

Tsugaru-kaikyō
Aomori
Hachinohe

Akita
Morioka
HONSHŪ
Yamagata
Sado-shima
Sendai
Noto-
hantō
Niigata
Fukushima
Kōriyama
Wajima
Nikkō
Toyama
Utsunomiya
Kanazawa
Nagano
Mito
Fukui
Maebashi
TŌKYŌ
Oki-
shotō
Takayama
Kofu
Matsue
Tottori
Nagoya
3376m
Chiba
Kyōto
Fuji-san
Yokohama
Kawasaki
Kōbe
Tsu
Shizuoka
Tsushima
Hiroshima
Ōsaka
Hamamatsu
Ō-shima
Yamaguchi
Okayama
Wakayama
Miyake-jima
Matsuyama
Tokushima
Kitakyūshū
Kōchi
Takamatsu
Hachijō-jima
Fukuoka
Kumamoto
Ōita
SHIKOKU
Nagasaki
1592m
Aso-san
Aoga-shima
KYŪSHŪ
Miyazaki
Kagoshima
Ōsumi-
shotō
Tane-ga-shima
Tori-shima

-shotō

Ogasawara-
guntō

Kazan-
rettō

Geography

*T*he traveller in Japan cannot fail to be aware that this is a land of islands and mountains. You are never far from the sea, while inland you are surrounded by impenetrable mountains, with tiny villages tucked into the folds. Japan's geography has a powerful effect on the life of its people. The landscape is ever changing, shaken by earthquakes or moulded by volcanic eruptions.

Landscapes

The Japanese call their island country Nippon, 'the root of the sun' or 'the land of the rising sun'. There are 3,922 islands in all (but four main ones), stretching like a necklace towards the Asian mainland, off the coast of Korea and China. A long narrow country, Japan extends from latitude 24°N to 45°N. Its northern part is parallel to Ottawa and Venice, the far south to Miami and the Sahara desert. From north to south it covers a distance of more than 3,000km, but from east to west you are never more than an hour's drive from the sea.

The result is a dramatic variety of landscape. The northernmost of the

major islands, Hokkaido is a land of rolling pastures, wide-open plains, deep gorges and rugged volcanic mountains. Most people live on the central and largest island, Honshu. Mountain ranges, covered in deep forest, run like a spine right down the centre of the island. They offer spectacular landscapes and fine skiing and hiking, but the land is largely uncultivable and uninhabitable. In the northwest is the Snow Country, a narrow coastal belt bordering the Sea of Japan, buried under snow two to three metres deep for nearly half the year. The space left for living is very small. Most people live crammed together on the flat land along Honshu's east – Pacific – coast. This is where the major cities are, as well as most industry and commerce.

The islands to the south, Shikoku and Kyushu, are semi-tropical. Shikoku is a quiet backwater of terraced paddy fields, orange groves and coral reefs. Lush Kyushu is dominated by two brooding volcanoes, Mount Aso and Mount Sakurajima. Further south still lie Okinawa and the Ryukyu islands, archetypal South Sea islands with white beaches and blue seas.

Restless earth

Geologically, Japan is a young country, still in the process of change. From north

A steam train puffs through the dramatic scenery formed by irrigated paddy fields

The spectacular volcanic landscape around Mount Aso forms the heart of Kyushu

to south there are volcanoes, many of them live: Mount Fuji, the most famous of all, perpetually trails a plume of smoke. Hot water, full of health-giving minerals, gushes from fissures in the rocks, forming natural hot springs. There are tremors nearly every day and from time to time a major earthquake such as the one that struck Kobe in 1995.

Climate

Because of Japan's latitude there are four distinct seasons, although large variations are experienced from north to south. Everyone will tell you that the best seasons to visit are spring and autumn. Spring, warm and dry, is cherry blossom time, while in late autumn everyone goes maple leaf viewing and the hills are a blaze of colour. Summer is hot and often humid (except in Hokkaido). Northern winters can be cold; elsewhere

temperatures tend to stay above freezing. See also page 181.

THOMAS COOK'S JAPAN
On 11 May 1874, Cook's *Excursionist and Tourist Advertiser contained the words: 'We ... have in contemplation the establishment of an agency in Japan.' By 1904 there was an annual spring tour by steamer and Pullman to 'the land of cherry blossom' and in 1906 the first office opened in Yokohama. The coronation of Emperor Taisho in 1915 inspired great interest. Cook's developed tours to the most remote parts of the country, reminding its travellers that for all its quaintness, Japan even in the 1920s was a fully westernised country: 'Even the humble cottage of the farmer in a remote village is lighted by electricity.'*

History

10,000-300BC
Jomon period. Early inhabitants of Japan produce rope-impressed pottery.
300BC-AD250
Yayoi period. The Yayoi people develop rice cultivation and use bronze and iron implements.
AD250-700
Kofun period. Large earthen tombs (*kofun*) built throughout Japan.
538-710
Asuka and Hakuho periods. Buddhism and Confucianism enter Japan from China.
710-94
Nara period. Nara becomes Japan's first capital. Flowering of culture.
794-1185
Heian period. Splendid new capital established in Kyoto (Heiankyo), which becomes the centre of an aesthetically refined aristocratic culture. Great advances in art, literature and religion. Murasaki Shikibu writes *The Tale of Genji* (c 1010). But gradually civilisation becomes decadent.
1192-1333
Kamakura period. Military rule. Yoritomo Minamoto becomes first shogun, establishing court in Kamakura. The emperors, mere figureheads, remain cloistered in Kyoto while a succession of warlords battle to control the country.

1274 and 1281
Mongol armadas under Kublai Khan try twice to invade Japan but are driven back by a storm or divine wind (*kami kaze*).
1336-1573
Ashikaga period. The Ashikaga shoguns rule from Kyoto. Building of Golden and Silver Pavilions, development of *noh* theatre. Civil war overtakes the country.
1543
Portuguese sailors are shipwrecked in southern Kyushu, the first Europeans to reach Japan. They introduce bread, cake, Christianity and firearms.
1573-1600
Using Portuguese-style guns, Nobunaga Oda defeats his rivals and unifies the country, but is assassinated by one of his own generals (1582). Toyotomi Hideyoshi succeeds him. Tokugawa Ieyasu defeats Hideyoshi's son at the Battle of Sekigahara (1600). Sen no Rikyu develops the tea ceremony.
1603-1868
Edo or Tokugawa period. Ieyasu makes himself shogun and ruler of all Japan. He moves his capital to Edo (Tokyo). The Tokugawa shoguns rule Japan, enforcing strict rules of conduct for every member of society and closing

1904: the cocky Japanese jack sparrow (Emperor Meiji) defeats the Russian bear

the country to foreigners. The result is peace and a flowering of culture, particularly among the merchants of Edo. Development of *haiku* poetry, *kabuki* and *bunraku* theatre and *ukiyo-e* woodblock prints.

1853
The American Commodore Matthew Perry steams into Yokohama Bay and demands that Japan open to trade with the west (commercial Treaty of Kanagawa signed 1858).

1868-1912
Meiji period. The last shogun is ousted. Emperor Meiji leaves Kyoto to establish his capital in Edo, renamed Tokyo. His reign is a period of extraordinary modernisation and change. Land reform and compulsory education are introduced and a new constitution adopted.

1904-5
Russo-Japanese War. Japan defeats Russia – Asia's first modern defeat of a European power.

1912-26
Taisho period. Reign of Emperor Taisho. The jazz age in Japan.

1923
The Great Earthquake levels Tokyo. More than 100,000 killed. The city is quickly rebuilt.

1926-89
Showa period. Reign of Emperor Hirohito (posthumously known as Emperor Showa). During the late 1920s and 1930s, the military gradually takes power in Japan. Japan occupies Korea, Taiwan and much of China and begins to build an empire in Asia.

1941
Japan attacks the US naval base at Pearl Harbor and enters World War II.

Memorial to Hiroshima atomic bomb victims

1945
Much of Tokyo destroyed by firebombs. The Americans drop atomic bombs on Hiroshima and Nagasaki. For the first time in its history Japan is defeated.

1945-52
The Americans under General Douglas MacArthur occupy Japan, provide aid to rebuild the country. New constitution (1946) gives more personal rights. Emperor renounces his divine descent.

1952
Occupation ends. Under Liberal Democratic Party (LDP), Japan concentrates on building up its economy.

1964
The Tokyo Olympics symbolise Japan's new-found prosperity.

1965-92
Japan becomes an economic superpower.

1990–present
Heisei period. Reign of Emperor Akihito. Economic downturn begins in 1992 and in 1993 LDP loses power for the first time in 38 years. A succession of coalition governments follows. The leader of the Social Democrats, Tomiichi Murayama, becomes prime minister in 1994, leading a coalition dominated by the LDP.

1995
Massive earthquake devastates Kobe, Japan's fifth city.

CASTLES AND SAMURAI

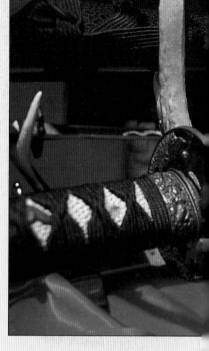

Dotted around Japan are castles, potent symbols of its samurai past. Some are perched on hilltops, others guard the centre of cities, protected by moats and surrounded by a maze of streets to foil the enemy invader.

The first castles were built as fortresses for the warlords who battled to control Japan in the Middle Ages. Then the Tokugawa shoguns took power and decreed that there should be just one castle in each province. This was where the *daimyo* – the warlord of the province – lived, though he was forced to make the long journey to Edo (Tokyo) every year to pay homage to the shogun.

The shoguns maintained peace by keeping strict control over the country.

They divided society into four classes: samurai (warriors), peasant farmers, artisans and merchants. The samurai were not allowed to work, but were supported by the taxes of the farming class. They carried two swords and had the right to lop off the head of any member of the lower classes who failed to treat them with due respect.

With no battles to fight and no work to do, the samurai developed the fighting arts to a high level of skill, ceremonial and ritual. They also practised tea

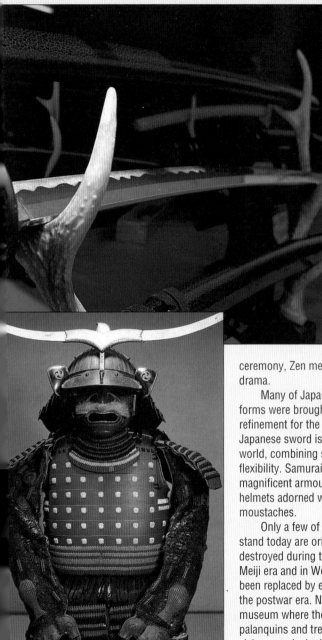

Arts of the warriors: the Japanese sword, pinnacle of the swordsmith's art; Himeji Castle; and a sword guard in the image of a samurai

ceremony, Zen meditation and *noh* drama.

Many of Japan's most exquisite art forms were brought to a peak of refinement for the samurai. The curved Japanese sword is the finest in the world, combining strength and flexibility. Samurai also sported magnificent armour, including fearsome helmets adorned with horns and moustaches.

Only a few of the castles which stand today are originals. Most were destroyed during the early years of the Meiji era and in World War II and have been replaced by exact replicas, built in the postwar era. Nearly all contain a museum where the swords, armour, palanquins and treasures of the local *daimyo* are lovingly displayed.

Culture

At a glance Japan seems like a mirror-image of the West: modern people drive modern cars and walk along modern streets; there is a Disneyland; McDonald's purvey burgers on every main street, and you can buy any imaginable variety of American ice-cream. Yet it is strangely, undeniably *different*. The Japanese themselves are obsessed with their uniqueness. Barely a week goes by without a new book coming out on what it means to be Japanese.

A shopper asks a mendicant monk for his blessing in central Kyoto

The Japanese versus the rest

Until 1853, Japan was a closed society. Despite nearly 150 years of contact with the outside world, it is still very insular. You will soon discover that you are a *gaijin*, an 'outside person'. You are therefore an honoured guest. The Japanese tradition of hospitality is very strong and you will be treated with great kindness. But you will never be allowed to forget that you are different; even westerners who speak perfect Japanese never cease to be *gaijin*.

All for one, one for all

Many people will tell you, 'We Japanese do this, we Japanese are like that ...' Japanese consider themselves primarily Japanese and only secondarily individuals. This does not mean that they have no individual thoughts and feelings. But in the last analysis they accept that their personal desires will often have to be put aside for the good of the group, be it their family, their company or society as a whole.

The dichotomy between doing your duty and your own desires is a fundamental theme in Japanese life and literature. A prime example is love. Most people still marry a suitable partner, approved of by their parents, and arranged marriage is surprisingly common. But a young person sometimes falls in love with someone completely 'unsuitable', and this can lead to tragedy.

Harmony

There is a Japanese saying: 'A nail that sticks up must be hammered down.' In a small island, crowded with people, the most important thing is to maintain harmony. As in many traditional societies, there are strict rules surrounding Japanese life. There is a well-ordered hierarchy: Japanese are expected to treat those above them with due respect and to follow their orders without questioning. Everyone – from the street cleaner to the head of a multi-national company – takes pride in his work and does the best he can.

Etiquette is very important. In almost any situation there is a proper way to behave. You take your shoes off at the door of the house; you bow 45, 60 or 90 degrees when you meet someone, depending on their status. Rules like this maintain the surface harmony of society, and if the surface is harmonious, the rest of society will be too. The traditional Japanese arts, such as tea ceremony, are all to do with establishing the form and getting it exactly right.

Breaking out

This does not mean that the Japanese do not have fun. For instance, in counterpoint to the Zen aesthetic of elegance and refinement, there are also exuberant Shinto festivals when everyone lets their hair down. In defiance of good taste some people fill their traditional homes with kitsch dolls and baubles, while the streets are decorated with plastic cherry blossoms or maple leaves (depending on the season) and the night is garish with glittering neon signs. In the subway, businessmen read pornographic comics ... and the offerings of Japanese television are frequently bizarre.

Street trade with a distinctly Japanese flavour: selling penny whistles in Hakone

After a hard day at the office obeying their superiors, men can go to the bar, get drunk, sit on the hostess's lap and tell their boss exactly what they think of him, without fear of repercussions. These are safety valves, accepted ways in which people can release all the pressure which their tight-knit society puts upon them.

Politics

*J*apanese politics is in a state of flux. For nearly 40 years the LDP (Liberal Democratic Party – conservative, despite the name) remained in power. Politics was a matter of infighting between rival factions within that party, with the other parties largely an irrelevance. Although it was superficially a democracy, in effect Japan functioned as a one-party state.

Today all that has changed. In 1993 the LDP finally fell from power and was replaced by a coalition government. Japan then had four prime ministers in the space of a year before the LDP once again took power – under a Socialist prime minister.

Japan's system of government is close to the British model. At the top is the emperor, a purely constitutional monarch. Below him is the Diet, made up of two houses, like the British parliament. Real decision-making power rests with the House of Representatives, elected every four years. The Upper House, known as the House of Councillors, is elected every six years.

The Iron Triangle

Power does not rest solely in the hands of politicians. The bureaucrats of key ministries, notably the Ministry of Finance and MITI (the Ministry of International Trade and Industry), wield much power. Big business, which funds the LDP and has great influence, forms the third side of the 'Iron Triangle'.

Recently the electorate has become more and more disgusted with the rampant corruption and political infighting of the LDP. There have been calls for reform. Despite its economic strength, Japan still plays only a small part in international affairs such as peace-keeping. There are demands that it should contribute more. With their economic base now secure, people are turning their attention to politics: Japan is likely to see great changes over the next few years.

Election posters, Kagoshima

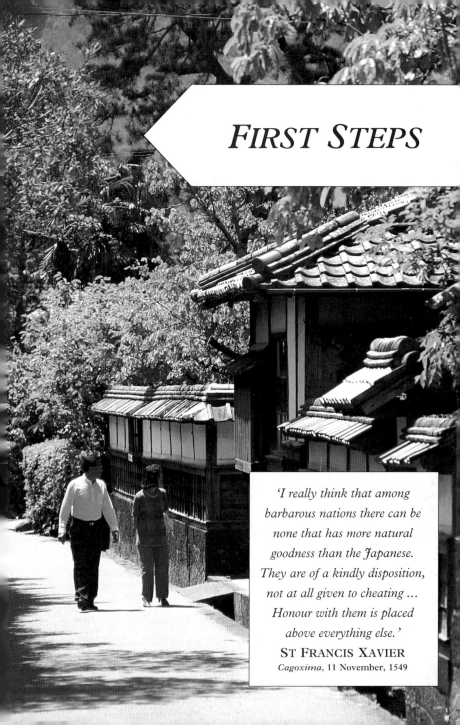

FIRST STEPS

'I really think that among
barbarous nations there can be
none that has more natural
goodness than the Japanese.
They are of a kindly disposition,
not at all given to cheating ...
Honour with them is placed
above everything else.'

ST FRANCIS XAVIER
Cagoxima, 11 November, 1549

First Steps

*I*n some ways Japan is like a large village. It is a safe, orderly society where women can, in the main, confidently walk alone down the darkest street in the middle of the night, and where lost wallets are handed in to the police and returned to their owners. All this, along with trains that run precisely on time, makes Japan an extremely pleasant and comfortable place to visit.

Language

Your first shock on arriving in Japan may be the language: signs are written in incomprehensible characters. Fortunately you will also find many in English – station signs, for example.

Most Japanese educated after World War II have studied English for years, but surprisingly few speak it with any fluency. If you need help, look for a student or businessman, then speak slowly and clearly. If you are not understood, write your request down. Most people are far more used to reading English than to hearing it spoken. Look out too for resident foreigners, of whom there are plenty in Japan. And try to pick up even just a few words of Japanese (see pages 184–5).

Etiquette

Japan runs like clockwork – partly because there is a proper way to behave in practically any situation. As a foreigner, you will not be expected to know or follow these rules. But there are some *faux pas* which are simply unthinkable. The hints below may save embarrassment.

In the home: When visiting a Japanese home or a Japanese-style inn, remove your shoes at the door when you arrive: shoes are for outdoors only. You use slippers to walk around inside, but before entering a *tatami*-matted room, remove

There are English signs in the most unexpected places: Enryakuji Temple, Mount Hiei, Kyoto

撮影厳禁
NO PHOTOGRAPH

Floor-level living has its own etiquette: temple restaurant in Hagi

these. *Tatami* (rice straw matting) is like furniture, used for sitting or sleeping, therefore you do not walk on it in slippers. At the toilet, remove your slippers, leave them outside the door and use the special plastic toilet slippers.

When sitting on the floor, remember that the feet are considered unclean; avoid pointing them at people. Women should kneel or tuck their feet to one side. Men may sit cross-legged.

The bath: In Japan, the bath is a ritual and the ultimate relaxation, not just a question of cleanliness. The Japanese take a bath every evening, usually before dinner. The basic thing to remember is that everyone shares the bath water. Do not soil it with soap or dirt; and never pull the plug. There will always be taps and bowls or a shower where you wash, scrub thoroughly and rinse off before finally stepping into the bath. Japanese baths are extremely hot. Sit very still to avoid scalding and you will feel refreshed and exuberant.

Mealtime etiquette: If you are dining with Japanese, never start to eat until everyone has raised their glass to say '*kampai!*' (cheers!). If you do not drink or do not want a particular sort of food, it is better to accept what is offered and not eat (or drink) it, rather than to make a fuss and refuse it.

Conversation: 'Yes' (*Hai, hai*) almost never means 'Yes, I agree'. It simply means 'Yes, I am listening'.

Other caveats: It is considered rude to sneeze or blow your nose in public; these noisy bodily functions are as offensive as belching. If it is unavoidable, turn aside and say 'Excuse me'.

Never express anger, no matter what the provocation. Always smile and remain calm. Shouting and throwing a tantrum is a sure sign of the barbarian foreigner. Effusive thanks and effusive apologies help to oil the wheels.

If you need to indicate something, gesture with the palm of the hand upwards. Never point.

Getting Around

*J*apanese public transport works with breathtaking efficiency. For longer distances most Japanese fly; in fact a return flight may work out cheaper than travelling by train. Trains are ultra-hi-tech, extremely smooth, and arrive so precisely on the dot that you can plan your schedule with split-second timing. Even the subways and buses follow timetables to the second.

Before you leave
The **Japan Rail (JR) Pass** is the bargain of the century. These must be bought outside Japan, are valid only for foreign tourists, and allow unlimited travel on JR trains, including most bullet trains, JR buses and some ferries. There are 7-, 14- and 21-day passes. Enquire at the Japan National Tourist Office (JNTO).

Intercity travel
Air: There is an extensive network of internal airlines linking all major cities. The main domestic carriers are Japan Airlines (JAL), All Nippon Airways (ANA) and Japan Air Systems (JAS).

Rail: Trains are categorised on the basis of speed – the faster it goes, the more it costs. Make full use of the English-language railway timetable issued free by the JNTO, and be sure to take an express, avoiding *futsu* (ordinary trains). Besides the JR, there are local private lines, often cheaper and more convenient (unless you have a JR Pass).

Your JR Pass allows you to make seat reservations free – advisable as trains are often full, particularly at peak seasons.

Driving
Be prepared to get lost on minor roads, but main roads are well signposted, in English and Japanese.

To hire a car you need an international driving licence – and probably assistance from a Japanese-speaker. **Nippon Rentacar** (tel: 03 3496 0919), affiliated with Hertz, has a wide drop-off network. Reservations can be made from abroad.

Car rental starts at Y10,000 for 24 hours. There is a very high toll to use the expressways – for a single person travelling alone, nearly as much as the bullet train fare. Petrol is not expensive.

The Japanese drive on the left and, except on expressways, very slowly. Beware of speed traps. The speed limit is 40kph on all but major intercity roads, and the police fine offenders on the spot. Hitch-hiking is not a Japanese custom, but Japan is one of the safest countries in the world in which to hitch.

Local transport
Subways: Most major cities have extensive subway systems. Buy a ticket from a vending machine: if in doubt about the price, take the cheapest ticket and pay the excess at the other end. Subways run until just after midnight.

Bus: Buses are complicated to use, but in some cities, like Kyoto, there is no alternative. The Kyoto JNTO issues a bus map. Usually you take a ticket as you board and pay when you leave. There is a change machine at the front of the bus.

Taxis: Don't expect your taxi driver to speak English or even to know where he

There are still trams in several Japanese cities: this one runs in Nagasaki

is going. It is best to carry a note of the address of your destination in Japanese, to show the driver. Fares are metered. There is no tipping.

Trams: Many provincial cities, such as Hakodate, Kumamoto and Nagasaki, have trams. These are slow, noisy but very cheap and follow a clear route.

Bicycles: Cycling is an excellent way to get around small local areas. Everyone uses bicycles – station cycle parks are always jam-packed. You are required to cycle on the pavement (where there is one), which means that you do not risk being mown down by lorries. Rent-a-cycle is frequently available, usually at or very near the station.

When to go

Most people say that the best seasons in Japan are spring and autumn (though every season has its beauties). Times to avoid are the three main holiday periods, when the whole of Japan seems to be on the move. Around New Year, during Golden Week (29 April to 5 May) and during the O-Bon holiday in early August, many people return to their family homes or go travelling. Public transport is fully booked and crammed with passengers, the roads out of town are jammed, and Tokyo becomes a ghost town.

Where to go

Most travellers stick to Tokyo and Kyoto, with maybe a side trip to Hiroshima or Takayama, but Japan is so safe and convenient and public transport is so good that there is no need to restrict yourself in this way. First get off the bullet train line, which inevitably runs through industrial Japan. Use your JR

> **THE WONDERFUL JAPANESE TOILET**
>
> In the countryside you will find some of the most primitive toilets you have ever seen, but Japan is also the land of the ultra-hi-tech toilet. Most modern homes have a computerised lavatory, with a heated toilet seat and a panel of buttons which operate the in-built bidet and blow-dry system. Ladies' toilets often have a machine which makes a loud flushing noise at the press of a button, drowning out other noises – a boon for the bashful. If you are seriously interested in toilets, Tokyo's INAX showroom has a constantly updated exhibition of the most state-of-the-art models

Pass and JNTO timetable to explore the wild volcanic landscapes of Hokkaido, the semi-tropical jungles of Kyushu, the

dense forests of Tohoku and the picture-perfect paddy fields and orange groves of Shikoku. Or do as the Japanese do, and make your journey an exploration of Japan's holy mountains by day and spas by night.

A colourful float at Kyoto's Gion Matsuri festival in July (see pages 158–9)

WHAT TO SEE

'Looking at Tokyo, one
sometimes wonders why the
Japanese went to all the trouble
of franchising a Disneyland in
the suburbs when the capital
itself is so superior a version.'

DONALD RICHIE
*A Lateral View, Essays on
contemporary Japan, 1987*

Tokyo

*Y*our first impression when you arrive in Tokyo will be of incredible life and energy. This seems to be a city rushing into the 21st century at an unstoppable pace. Old buildings disappear, new ones spring up, parks and green spaces blossom. The streets throng with smart, fashionable people and are resplendent with glossy shops and expensive cars.

But this is only one face of Tokyo, the world's second largest city. Explore and you will find old neighbourhoods where the alleys are wide enough only for a bicycle. You will find temples and shrines even in the middle of bustling business districts, and gardens where you can escape from the busy streets.

As a capital, Tokyo has a very short history. When Ieyasu Tokugawa (see page 68) arrived in the village of Edo in 1590, it was no more than a few fishing huts and a tumbledown castle. He made it his powerbase and ruled the country from here as all-powerful shogun. In 1868, after the last shogun had been ousted, the Emperor Meiji moved to Edo, which was renamed Tokyo, the Eastern Capital. The city has suffered fires, earthquakes and the fire bombing of World War II, so there are few historic monuments to be seen. But the spirit of old Edo is still alive.

The best way to experience Tokyo is on foot: though a giant of a city, it's perfectly safe.

Dialling code: 03
Tourist Information Centre (TIC), 1-6-6 Yurakucho, Chiyoda-ku (tel: 3502 1461).

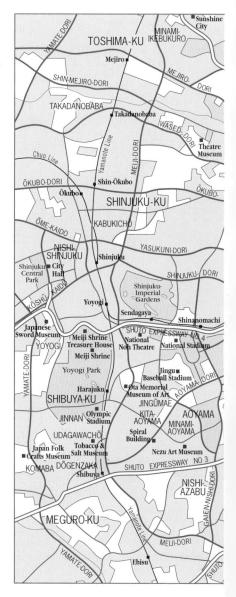

TOKYO CITY

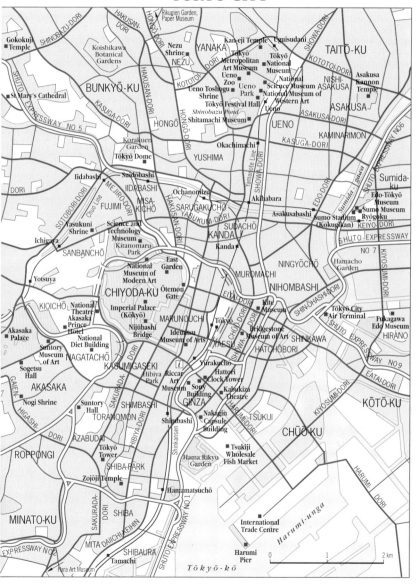

Neighbourhood Tokyo

*T*okyo is a city of neighbourhoods. Each has its own heart, its own logic and a unique character. One of the best ways of getting to grips with the giant maze that is Tokyo is to choose a neighbourhood and then roam around it.

AKASAKA

Akasaka's narrow streets are lined with bars, restaurants and nightclubs, and the whole area is bordered by high-class hotels and the TBS television headquarters. The limousines which jam the streets do not stop at the neon-lit bars but draw up at silent houses between them, hidden behind sand-coloured walls and closed gates. These are the city's classiest geisha houses, where politicians, industrialists and their guests enjoy fine Japanese cuisine and the attentions of elegant 'geisha' – literally 'arts people' (see page 83).
Southwest of Imperial Palace (subways: Akasaka-mitsuke, Akasaka).

ASAKUSA

Asakusa is the heart of old Edo, Tokyo's East End. In the days of the shogun, while the *daimyo* and samurai had their mansions in the hills now circled by the Yamanote rail line, Asakusa was where the merchants and craftsmen lived. Here they developed a lively culture, which grew all the more lively when the shogun banished the Yoshiwara pleasure quarters to the area. Few of the old buildings still stand, but the noisy, chaotic, downtown atmosphere remains.
Northeast Tokyo (subway: Asakusa); or by water bus from Hamamatsucho station or Hama Rikyu Gardens (see page 42).

GINZA

The Ginza is synonymous with glamour, sophistication and big-city living. Japan's most famous shopping district, it is full of glossy department stores and restaurants, art galleries, theatres and cinemas. The San'ai Building, on Ginza crossing, stands on the most expensive piece of land in the world. On Sundays the main street is closed to traffic and packed with pedestrians and pavement cafés.
10 minutes' walk southeast of Imperial Palace (subway: Ginza).

ROPPONGI

Roppongi comes alive in the evening, when youthful pleasure-seekers, all dressed to kill, head for the district's innumerable discos, clubs, bars or restaurants, or simply parade the main street. It is the most cosmopolitan part of the city, the haunt of glamorous characters of every nationality – foreign models, reggae bands ... While Roppongi caters to youth, the more sophisticated nightlife area is further west, in the **Nishi Azabu** and **Aoyama** districts.
Southwest of the Palace (subway: Roppongi).

SHIBUYA

Shibuya's rambling streets abound with shoppers, boutiques and fashion stores. One stop up the line in **Harajuku**, the crowds are even younger and the fashion more outrageous (see page 44).
In the west of the city (station: Shibuya).

SHINJUKU

Shinjuku's two wildly contrasting faces epitomise the extremes of Tokyo living.

On the west of the tracks is Japan's answer to Manhattan, full of gleaming modern skyscrapers dominated by Kenzo Tange's granite and glass City Hall (see page 32). Cross to the east side and you find yourself in a warren of streets crammed with shops and boutiques. Leave the main road and you plunge into the seedy alleys of **Kabukicho**, with strip joints, massage parlours and plenty more. This being Japan, the area is not dangerous, though it is sensible to be a little wary if you wander there at night.
In the west of the city (station: Shinjuku).

UENO

Most people come to Ueno for its park, which contains some of the country's finest museums, a zoo, amusement park and Shinobazu Pond, busy with waterfowl. It is also worth wandering Ueno's streets, bustling with stalls and small shops. **Yanaka**, to the north of Ueno, is one of the best-preserved parts of old Tokyo, with narrow lanes and wooden houses, temples and shops.
In the northeast of the city (station: Ueno).

Chuo-dori, the main street of the Ginza, packed on Sundays

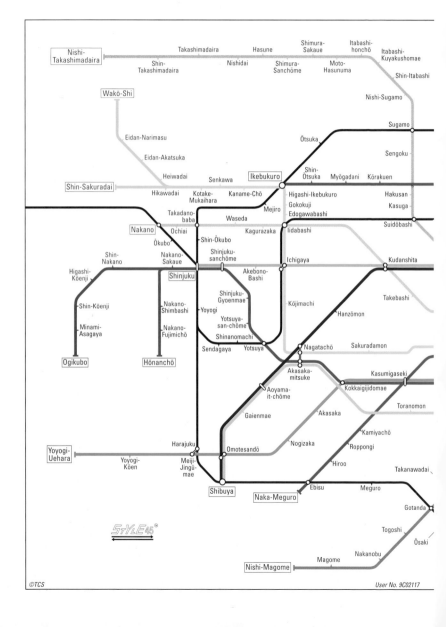

Nishi-Takashimadaira

Takashimadaira | Hasune | Shimura-Sakaue | Itabashi-honchō | Itabashi-Kuyakushomae
Shin-Takashimadaira | Nishidai | Shimura-Sanchōme | Moto-Hasunuma | Shin-Itabashi

Wakō-Shi

Nishi-Sugamo

Eidan-Narimasu

Ōtsuka

Sugamo

Eidan-Akatsuka

Sengoku

Heiwadai | Senkawa | Ikebukuro | Shin-Ōtsuka | Myōgadani | Kōrakuen

Shin-Sakuradai

Hikawadai | Kotake-Mukaihara | Kaname-Chō | Higashi-Ikebukuro | Hakusan
Gokokuji | Kasuga
Takadano-baba | Waseda | Mejiro | Edogawabashi

Nakano | Ochiai | Kagurazaka | Iidabashi | Suidōbashi

Ōkubo | Shin-Ōkubo

Shin-Nakano | Nakano-Sakaue | Shinjuku-sanchōme | Ichigaya | Kudanshita

Higashi-Kōenji | Shinjuku | Akebono-Bashi

Shin-Kōenji | Shinjuku-Gyoenmae | Kōjimachi | Takebashi
Nakano-Shimbashi | Yoyogi | Hanzōmon
Minami-Asagaya | Nakano-Fujimichō | Yotsuya-san-chōme
Shinanomachi

Ogikubo | Hōnanchō | Sendagaya | Yotsuya | Nagatachō | Sakuradamon

Akasaka-mitsuke | Kasumigaseki

Aoyama-it-chōme | Kokkaigijidomae

Toranomon

Gaienmae | Akasaka

Kamiyachō

Yoyogi-Uehara | Harajuku | Omotesandō | Nogizaka | Roppongi
Yoyogi-Kōen | Meiji-Jingū-mae | Hiroo
Takanawadai

Shibuya | Naka-Meguro | Ebisu | Meguro

Gotanda

Togoshi

Ōsaki

Nakanobu

Nishi-Magome | Magome

TRANSPORT

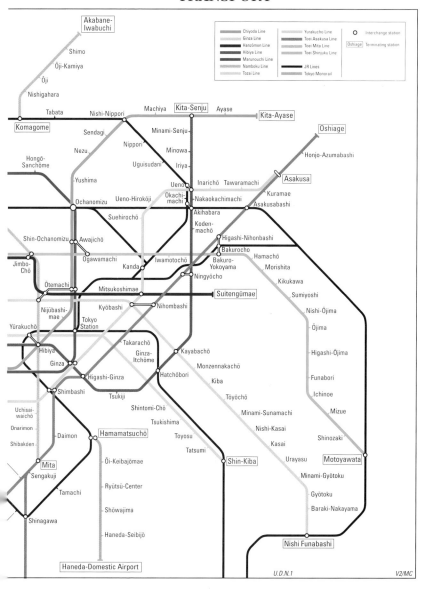

A glimpse of old Tokyo: the five-storey pagoda at Asakusa Kannon Temple

ASAKUSA KANNON TEMPLE

More than anywhere Asakusa Kannon (also called Sensoji) preserves the flavour of old Tokyo with its bustling medieval atmosphere. The temple, Tokyo's oldest and best loved, was founded in 628 when two brothers miraculously found a golden image of Kannon, the deity of compassion, in their fishing nets. This is no solemn house of worship. Pass Kaminarimon (Thunder Gate), with its twin gods of thunder and wind, and you come to Nakamise Street, a noisy arcade jammed with pilgrims, visitors and shopkeepers. The temple courtyard, alive with flapping pigeons, is lined with fortune-telling booths. The vast temple, a postwar reconstruction, houses the statue of Kannon, hidden within a gold-plated shrine (see also pages 42 and 43).

10 minutes' walk north of Asakusa station.

Tel: 3842 0181. Temple always open. Admission free.

KOKYO (Tokyo Imperial Palace)

The Imperial Palace is the still centre at the heart of Tokyo. The home of the emperor and his family, the palace itself is hidden deep inside a large impregnable expanse of woods and gardens. The public may enter only twice a year: at New Year (2 January, 9.30am–3pm) and on the Emperor's birthday (23 December, 8.30–11am), when the emperor appears and waves to the crowds.

This is where Tokyo began. The shogun built his castle here, the largest in the world, and the city expanded around it. The site of the castle is now the East Garden, which is open to the public. Some guardhouses and fortified turrets remain, together with the massive ramparts, built with huge slabs of volcanic rock shipped from Izu, 100km away.

You can also walk around the palace grounds. The most famous view is across Nijubashi Bridge, to Fushimi Tower rising above the walls. Or look down into the grounds from the observation floor of the 36-storey Kasumigaseki Building in nearby Toranomon.

2 minutes' walk west of Otemachi subway, 5 minutes' walk from Tokyo station. East Garden open: 9am–4pm, last entry 3pm; closed Monday, Friday. Admission free.

MEIJI JINGU (Meiji Shrine)

Meiji Shrine is dedicated to Emperor Meiji, who presided over Japan's transformation from a feudal country to a modern state. The shrine was completed in 1920, as a memorial both to him and his empress. You enter the peaceful wooded grounds through one of the largest wooden *torii* (gateway to a Shinto shrine) in the country, and stroll along shady gravel paths to the shrine buildings, rebuilt to the original design in 1958 after World War II destruction. Built from Japanese cypress, they are grand, dignified and timeless. In the grounds is the Iris Garden, where Meiji and his empress used to stroll; in June more than 100 varieties of iris bloom. In the first three days of January, millions of people visit to make their New Year wishes.

Harajuku station or Meiji Jingumae subway. Tel: 3379 5511. Shrine and inner garden open: sunrise to sunset. Admission free. Iris Garden open: 9am–4.30pm, 1 March to 3 November, 9am–4pm in winter. Admission charge.

UENO TOSHOGU SHRINE

Tucked away in a quiet corner of Ueno Park (see page 27), behind the zoo, is a shrine to Shogun Ieyasu Tokugawa, who unified Japan and founded Tokyo, and whose family dominated the country for 250 years. Completed in 1651, it is in the same lavish style as the Toshogu Shrine at Nikko (see page 68) and is the only shrine in Tokyo designated a 'National Treasure'. The dragons carved on the gateposts and the four paintings of animals within the shrine are by famous 17th-century artists.

10 minutes' walk west of Ueno station. Tel: 3822 3455. Open: daily, 9am–5.30pm, 9am–4.30pm in winter. Admission charge.

The impressive moat and bridge of the Imperial Palace, home of the emperor

MODERN ARCHITECTURE

Japan, with its concrete streets, modern buildings and glittering neon nightscapes, is an extraordinary place for an architect to work. There are virtually no planning regulations and buildings have an expected life of little more than 10 years. Architects have an unusual degree of freedom – which results in some stunning creations and many truly wacky and outrageous buildings.

The grand old man of Japanese architecture is Kenzo Tange, whose 48-storey granite and glass City Hall (1991) towers over the Shinjuku skyline. His masterpiece was the dramatic Yoyogi Stadium, built for the Tokyo Olympics in 1964 (see page 44). Tanze was also responsible for the glass-fronted Sogetsu Hall in Aoyama (1977) and the soaring pleated façade of the Akasaka Prince Hotel (1983).

Other great names in Tokyo architecture include Fumihiko Maki (look for his graceful Spiral Building in Omotesando) and Kisho Kurokawa,

responsible for some of Japan's wittiest and most provocative buildings, such as the Nakagin Capsule Building (1972) in Shimbashi, Tokyo, and the Sony Tower (1976) in Osaka's Shinsaibashi; both can be dismantled and reassembled when their units become obsolete.

Several of Japan's most innovative architects are based outside Tokyo. Osaka is the home of Tadao Ando and contains several of his understated and beautifully-structured buildings, in textured,

highly-polished concrete. But Osaka's most spectacular sight is the glowing white towers of Kirin Plaza (1988) on Ebisu Bridge, surrounded by throbbing neon. This futuristic marble building featured in Ridley Scott's film *Black Rain* and was designed by Kyoto-based Shin Takamatsu, whom many consider Japan's most exciting young architect.

Foreign architects too have contributed to the dazzling mosaic of the Japanese cityscape. In Tokyo, look for British architect Sir Norman Foster's Century Tower (1991) in Omotesando; in Asakusa, it is impossible to miss French designer Philippe Starck's amiably absurd Flamme d'Or (see page 42).

(see page 42).

Tokyo's glittering façades: Starck's Flamme d'Or; Tange's City Hall, and the Shinjuku skyline

Tokyo Gardens

Tokyo contains several exquisite landscaped gardens that are a legacy of the rule of the shoguns, when every *daimyo* (feudal lord) had to maintain a mansion in Edo (old Tokyo). Besides the gardens described below, other oases of green include the Imperial Palace East Garden and Meiji Shrine Outer Garden (see pages 30–1), Ueno Park (see page 27) and Yoyogi Park (see page 45).

HAMA RIKYU GARDENS (Hama Detached Palace Gardens)

These beautiful gardens border the River Sumida and have a small lake whose waters ebb and flow with the tides; a teahouse stands on stilts in the middle. Winding paths lead to tiny hillocks, from which you can supposedly see Mount Fuji. The gardens once belonged to the shoguns and later to the imperial family.

10 minutes' walk south of Shimbashi station. Tel: 3541 0200. Open: 9am–4.30pm, last entry 4pm; closed Monday. Admission charge.

RIKUGIEN GARDEN

Rikugien's gravelled paths meander around a lake, crossed with bridges and overhung with exquisitely trimmed pine trees. Designed and laid out by the *daimyo* Yoshiyasu Yanagisawa around 1700, the garden re-creates 88 scenic spots mentioned in Chinese and Japanese poetry.

10 minutes' walk south of Komagome station. Tel: 3941 2222. Open: 9am–5pm, last entry 4.30pm; closed Monday. Admission charge.

SHINJUKU GYOEN (Shinjuku Imperial Gardens)

The rolling lawns of Shinjuku Gyoen are where Tokyoites go to relax on hot summer days. Once the estate of a *daimyo* family, it was made into a park in the Meiji period, when Japan was absorbing many influences from the west. Besides the western-style lawns, there are lakes, a Japanese garden with a teahouse, and a formal French landscape garden with rose beds and clipped hedges.

5 minutes' walk south of Shinjuku Gyoenmae subway. Tel: 3350 0151. Open: 9am–4.30pm, last entry 4pm; closed Monday. Admission charge.

A perfect lotus flower on display in the poetic Rikugien Garden

Tokyo Museums

Tokyo is a treasure-house of museums. There are the huge public collections such as the Tokyo National Museum, the finest collection of Japanese art in the world; tiny museums lovingly devoted to just one thing, such as swords, kites or paper; and many fine and idiosyncratic collections assembled by business magnates who invested their fortunes in art. Several fascinating museums are devoted to the history of Edo, with streets of wooden buildings and audio-visual evocations of Edo life taking you back to old Tokyo. Note that most museums are closed on Mondays.

EDO-TOKYO HAKUBUTSUKAN (Edo-Tokyo Museum)

This splendid museum opened in March 1993. In the heart of downtown Tokyo, next to the sumo stadium, it celebrates the life and history of the city of Tokyo, from its founding in the 16th century to the present. You enter the museum via a replica of Nihombashi Bridge (from where every distance in Japan is measured) and walk between full-scale models of old Edo/Tokyo buildings – a *kabuki* theatre, a newspaper office, and downtown shops and homes. There are displays devoted to samurai, townspeople, the pleasure quarters, the great earthquake and the war.
At Ryogoku station. Tel: 3626 9974. Open: 10am–6pm, 10am–9pm on Friday; closed Monday. Admission charge.

FUKAGAWA EDO SHIRYOKAN (Fukagawa Edo Museum)

It is worth the 15-minute stroll through the backstreets of downtown Tokyo to reach this charming small museum. Still

Haniwa: a terracotta burial figure, one of the exhibits in the National Museum

fairly new, it re-creates a whole neighbourhood of old Edo (17th–19th century Tokyo). Old shops and houses, which you can walk inside, are pressed roof to roof along narrow, earthen-floored alleys. There is a fire tower, an outdoor marketplace, and a river where the sun rises and sets at regular intervals.
15 minutes' walk north of Monzennakacho subway. Tel: 3630 8625. Open: daily, 10am–5pm. Admission charge.

HARA BIJUTSUKAN (Hara Art Museum)

The Hara is the only museum in the city devoted to contemporary art. Founded by Toshio Hara in 1979, it occupies his striking 1938 Bauhaus-style family residence. There are three or four major exhibitions a year, showcasing leading postwar international and Japanese artists of the stature of Christo Javacheff (the New York artist famous for his 'wrapped buildings'), and an annual spring show of work by young Japanese artists. In the garden is a café designed by internationally renowned architect Arata Isozaki.

10 minutes' walk west of Kita-Shinagawa station, 15 minutes' walk south of Shinagawa station. Tel 3445 0651. Open: 11am–5pm; closed Monday and while changing exhibitions. Admission charge.

IDEMITSU BIJUTSUKAN (Idemitsu Museum of Art)

This museum houses one of the finest collections of classical Japanese and Chinese art in Tokyo, acquired by the oil tycoon Sazo Idemitsu (though only a small selection is on display at any one time). It includes superb examples of Chinese and Japanese ceramics, ancient screens and painted scrolls, lacquerware and bronzes. Idemitsu's particular passion was for the wild, inspired ink paintings of the 17th-century Zen artist Sengai: the museum owns nearly all in existence. It also has one of the best views in Tokyo, right over the Imperial Palace.

5 minutes' walk from Yurakucho subway, 10 minutes' walk north of Hibiya subway, Yurakucho station. Tel: 3213 9402. Open: 10am–5pm, last entry 4.30pm; closed Monday. Admission charge.

KAGAKU GIJUTSUKAN (Science and Technology Museum)

This is a hands-on science museum where visitors can interact with every exhibit, the perfect place to take children on a rainy day. They can ride in a spaceship, an earthquake simulator or a time machine, play with new computer programmes and learn about iron, energy, plastics or electricity.

10 minutes' walk west of Takebashi subway. Tel: 3212 8471. Open: daily, 9.30am–4.50pm, last entry 4pm. Admission charge.

KAMI NO HAKUBUTSUKAN (Paper Museum)

The Chinese invented paper, but the Japanese turned it into an artform: craftsmen create *washi*, exquisitely fine paper made from mulberry bark; paper is folded to make origami; and doors and windows of traditional houses are made from paper. The Paper Museum celebrates all these.

2 minutes' walk from Oji station. Tel: 3911 3545. Open: 9.30am–4.30pm, last entry 4pm; closed Monday. Admission charge.

KORITSU KAGAKU HAKUBUTSUKAN (National Science Museum)

Five large halls are devoted to all kinds of science. There are dinosaurs and a section on the evolution of the Japanese people, as well as a working model of the 'maglev', the futuristic magnetically levitated railway, and a flight simulator where you can try out your skills as a pilot.

5 minutes' walk north of Ueno station. Tel: 3822 0111. Open: 9am–4.30pm, last entry 4pm; closed Monday. Admission charge.

NEZU BIJUTSUKAN (Nezu Institute of Fine Arts)

This famous art museum was founded by the railway magnate Kaichiro Nezu in 1940, and houses his magnificent collection of Asian art. In all there are 7,000 pieces, though only a few are on display at any one time. The collection includes Gandharan sculptures from 4th-century Pakistan; Chinese bronzes, monochrome landscape paintings and music-box clocks; and a wonderful collection of Buddhist sculptures from the earliest periods of Japanese art. The most famous exhibits are a 13th-century painting of Nachi Waterfall and a 17th-century gold screen painted with irises. The museum itself is set in a beautiful wooded garden, dotted with stone lanterns and tea ceremony huts.

10 minutes' walk south of Omotesando subway. Tel: 3400 2536. Open: 9.30am–4.30pm, last entry 4pm; closed Monday. Admission charge.

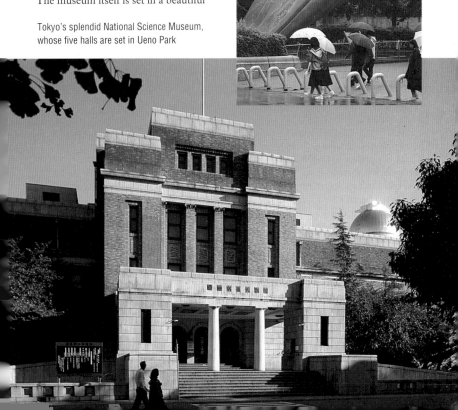

Tokyo's splendid National Science Museum, whose five halls are set in Ueno Park

Samurai armour in the Tokyo National Museum evokes a feudal past

NIHON MINGEIKAN (Japan Folk Craft Museum)

This is a wonderful collection of folkcrafts – stoneware pots, indigo-dyed fabrics, heavy wooden furniture – assembled by the folk-art patron and author Yanagi Soetsu, and lovingly displayed in a fine old farmhouse, brought piece by piece from the country and reconstructed here.
10 minutes' west of Komaba Todaimae station. Tel: 3467 4527. Open: 10am–5pm, last entry 4pm; closed Monday. Admission charge.

OTA KINEN BIJUTSUKAN (Ota Memorial Museum of Art)

This small, tranquil museum in the heart of noisy Harajuku houses a fine collection of *ukiyo-e* (Japanese woodblock prints), assembled by the business tycoon Seizo Ota. The 12,000 works include many by Hokusai, Hiroshige and other masters of the art. Only a few are on show at any one time.
5 minutes' walk from Meiji Jingumae subway. Tel: 3403 0880. Open: 10.30am–5.30pm, last entry 5pm; closed Monday and 25th to end of each month. Admission charge.

RICCAR BIJUTSUKAN (Riccar Art Museum)

An extensive collection of *ukiyo-e* woodblock prints, rotated for viewing in a tiny gallery in the heart of Ginza.

5 minutes' walk east of Ginza subway. Tel: 3571 3254. Open: 11am–6pm; closed Monday. Admission charge.

SHITAMACHI FUZOKU SHIRYOKAN (Shitamachi Museum)

This is the first of the museums built to preserve the flavour of old Edo/Tokyo (Shitamachi means 'downtown'). On the ground floor are old shops and houses, including a merchant's house and a sweet shop; upstairs is a jumble of everyday utensils, toys and knick-knacks.

5 minutes' walk south of Ueno station and subway. Tel: 3823 7451. Open: 9.30am–4.30pm; closed Monday. Admission charge.

SUMO HAKUBUTSUKAN (Sumo Museum)

Sumo enthusiasts will not want to miss this sumo hall of fame, next to the Kokugikan, the sumo stadium, where you can admire the champions' embroidered trappings and look at woodblock prints of past heroes.

2 minutes' walk north of Ryogoku station. Tel: 3622 0366. Open: 9.30am–4.30pm; closed Saturday and Sunday. Admission free.

TABAKO TO SHIO NO HAKUBUTSUKAN (Tobacco and Salt Museum)

Idiosyncratic but interesting, the museum houses a collection of artefacts showing the history of smoking, from Mayan times onwards. There is also a floor devoted to salt, from a pillar of salt to models of Japanese salt farms.

15 minutes' walk north of Shibuya station. Tel: 3476 2041. Open: 10am–6pm, last entry 5.30pm; closed Monday. Admission charge.

TAKO NO HAKUBUTSUKAN (Kite Museum)

This fascinating museum devoted to the wonderful Japanese kite contains 3,000 examples squeezed into its tiny space. And you can watch the curator making yet another.

2 minutes' walk from Nihombashi subway. Tel: 3275 2704. Open: 11am–5pm; closed Sunday. Admission charge.

TOKYO KOKURITSU HAKUBUTSUKAN (Tokyo National Museum)

You can get some idea of the incredible wealth, variety and tradition of Japanese art and culture from the best collection in the world, here in the country's finest museum. The main building is devoted to superb examples from every field of Japanese art: painting, from ancient mandalas to woodblock prints; sculpture, including 7th- and 8th-century Buddhas and modern works; ceramics, textiles, swords, lacquerware, *inro* (medicine boxes) and exquisitely carved *netsuke* (belt toggles). Don't miss the magnificent collection of prehistoric and proto-historic art in the Meiji-period Hyokeikan building, including Jomon-period earthenware, bug-eyed figurines and *haniwa*, terracotta images of people, houses and animals from tomb burials.

If you visit the museum on a fine Thursday, you may be able to see the priceless treasures of religious art displayed in the Horyuji Treasure House (it is closed when the weather is rainy or humid).

10 minutes' walk north of Ueno station. Tel: 3822 1111. Open: 9.30am–4.30pm, last entry 4pm; closed Monday. Admission charge.

Tokyo Environs

Some of Japan's most glorious natural scenery and famous hot spring resorts are within easy reach of Tokyo. Make sure you visit off season, or you will find yourself in company with thousands of others.

ATAMI

Along with Beppu (see page 132), Atami is one of the most famous and popular spas in Japan. For hot spring *aficionados* it is a must – but be prepared for noise, souvenir shops, amusement arcades and all the trappings of commercialism.
1 hour southwest of Tokyo by train.

FUJI-SAN AND FUJI GO-KO
(Mount Fuji and the Fuji Five Lakes)

The sublime cone of Mount Fuji, soaring magically from what appears to be a flat plain, has inspired poets and artists for centuries. At 3,776m, it is the highest mountain in Japan and a still-active volcano: from time to time there are rumbles, and the most recent eruption was in 1707. Fuji is notoriously shy and very often hidden behind a veil of cloud,

but on a fine day you can see it from Tokyo. There are good views from the bullet train, from Hakone and from the lakes at its base.

The Fuji Five Lakes region is a popular resort area for Tokyoites. Lake Yamanaka is a rich man's playground, with golf courses, watersports and villas. Kawaguchi is the most accessible, Lake Saiko is famous for its mysterious lava caves, and Lake Motosu is the deepest. The prettiest is Lake Shoji, surrounded by wooded hills on three sides, with a beautiful view of Fuji soaring above the trees. (For information on climbing Fuji, see page 52.)
2½ hours west of Tokyo by bus; or train to Lake Kawaguchi, then bus.

HAKONE

On holiday weekends, Tokyoites flock to Hakone. It has craggy peaks, a serene lake, thermal hot waters aplenty, an atmospheric turn-of-the-century hotel and wonderful views of Mount Fuji. Despite all this it is still relatively unspoilt, particularly if you go out of season (see also page 54).
1½ hours southwest of Tokyo by train.

IZU

The epicentre of past earthquakes that have flattened Tokyo, the Izu Peninsula has romantic crags, misty valleys and a plethora of hot spring resorts. Shimoda,

The mystical form of Mount Fuji, seen from the Izu Peninsula

TOKYO ENVIRONS

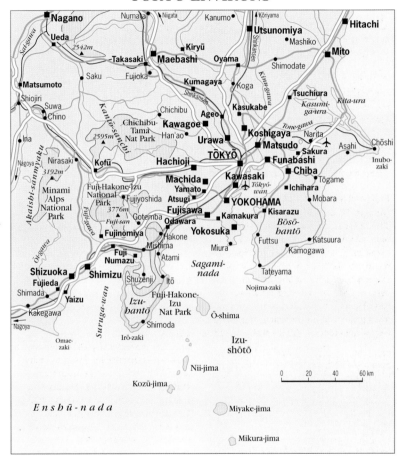

at the tip of the peninsula, is a pretty town with many picturesque plaster-walled houses. It is famous as the port through which the first westerners entered Japan. Commodore Perry arrived here with his Black Ships in 1854, an event commemorated in the annual Black Ships Festival in May. The first American consul, Townsend Harris, established his consulate here and had an affair with a geisha named Okichi. Izu's most famous spa is Shuzenji, a placid town with a river running through the centre, overhung with willows and crossed by red bridges.

Southwest of Tokyo, beyond Atami.
Shimoda and Shuzenji accessible by road and rail, most of the peninsula only by road.

Downtown Tokyo

This stroll through the heart of old Tokyo takes in the city's oldest and best loved temple and also one of the brashest symbols of the modern city. The tour can be topped or tailed depending on time. Bear in mind that Dembo-in Garden closes at 3pm. *Allow 3 to 5 hours.*

Start at Hama Rikyu Gardens, near Shimbashi station. If time is short, begin at Azuma Bridge (subway: Asakusa).

1 HAMA RIKYU GARDENS

At Hama Rikyu Gardens (see page 34), board the water bus which departs about every 40 minutes for Asakusa to go up the River Sumida, under a succession of bridges, past modern high-rise buildings crammed next to wooden temples and geisha houses. Finally to your right you see Philippe Starck's gleaming Flamme d'Or.

Alight at Azuma Bridge.

2 AZUMA-BASHI (Azuma Bridge)

Before starting your walk, admire the outrageous Flamme d'Or, a beer hall and restaurant built for the Asahi beer company (you could even drop in for a drink).

Cross the main road in front of you and take the covered shopping street. On your right you come to a large wooden gateway, Kaminarimon.

3 NAKAMISE-DORI (Nakamise Street)

Kaminarimon (Thunder Gate), a reconstruction of the original which burnt down in 1865, bears the thunder god (right) and the wind god (left). Walk through into Nakamise-dori, lined with stalls selling anything that might appeal to the daily crowds of pilgrims who pass through, from trinkets to *happi* coats (blue cotton workmen's jackets), oiled umbrellas and freshly baked rice crackers.

At the end of Nakamise-dori you come to another great gateway, Hozo-mon, and Asakusa Kannon Temple.

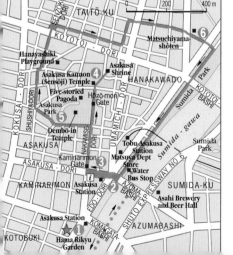

4 ASAKUSA KANNON TEMPLE

After exploring the temple and the temple grounds (see page 30), visit the fine old 17th-century Asakusa jinja (shrine). Then go to the office at the foot of the five-storey pagoda and ask to see Dembo-in. Sign the visitors' book and you will be given a ticket and a map.

Retrace your steps down Nakamise-dori and take the first turning on the right. To your right is a large temple gate leading to Dembo-in.

5 DEMBO-IN

A peaceful retreat, Dembo-in is the residence of the abbot of Asakusa Kannon. The 17th-century garden with its large pond, home to many turtles, has beautiful views of the five-storey pagoda.

Pilgrims and tourists flock to the Asakusa Kannon Temple: incense is burned in the centre

Continue along the road to your right to a wide street lined with cinemas, strip joints and game parlours (Shushiya-dori). This used to be the entertainment centre of Tokyo – Japan's first cinema was built here in 1903, and people flocked to see movies, cabaret and music-hall. There are still plenty of cinemas, with lurid billboards outside.

Return via the shopping arcades to Asakusa station. Or stroll on to the end of the road, to the Moorish towers of Hanayashiki playground. Walk through the arcade, then cross the main road, turn right down the first side road and cut through the back streets towards the river to a small temple on a hill.

6 MATSUCHIYAMA-SHOTEN

Dedicated to marital bliss and prosperity, this is where young blades would wait for the boat to the pleasure quarters.

Return to Asakusa subway along the riverside, through Sumida Park with its cherry trees.

Dembo-in – Open: 9am–3pm; closed Sunday. Admission free.
Matsuchiyama-shoten – Open: 6am–4.30pm; closed Sunday. Admission free.

Modern Tokyo

This walk takes you through some of the city's busiest and most fashionable streets. It is full of interest any day of the week but best of all on Sundays, when strolling the streets of Shibuya is practically a Tokyo institution.
Allow 3 hours.

At Shibuya station, take the Hachiko exit.

1 SHIBUYA

The most famous meeting place in Tokyo is the statue of Hachiko the dog, in the station square. The real Hachiko waited patiently every day at the station for many years after his master died, the perfect example of the faithful dog. Roads radiate in every direction, while the huge Sony screen opposite bombards shoppers with images and advertisements.
Cross the road and walk north past Seibu department store. Turn left on to Koen-dori.

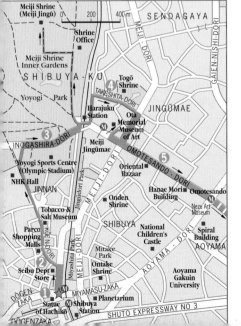

2 KOEN-DORI (Park Street)

Park Street is full of chic young people sauntering up and down. To the left is a succession of extraordinary stores, starting with the brutal new Humax Building (housing cinemas), followed by Loft (hi-tech knick-knacks), Wave (CDs and tapes), Seed (fashions) and Parco (more fashions). The small back streets behind Parco are worth exploring too. Beyond Parco is the Tobacco and Salt Museum (see page 39), while at the top the street opens on to the magnificent Yoyogi Sports Centre (Olympic Stadium, see page 32).
Cross the road and walk straight on, keeping the stadium to your right. At the end of the road turn right along the edge of Yoyogi Park.

3 YOYOGI-KOEN PERIMETER ROAD (Inogashira-dori)

This street runs along the side of Yoyogi

Park, one of Tokyo's largest stretches of green. On fine Sundays it shudders to the beat of heavy metal and rock 'n' roll, blasting out of a hundred amplifiers. Teddy boys in winklepickers and black leather gyrate next to teenage girls dancing solemnly in formation. The scene is among the capital's most inexplicable and extraordinary phenomena.

At the end of the road turn left to explore Meiji Shrine (see pages 30–1). Leave the shrine by the same gate. Turn left to pass Harajuku station – one of Tokyo's oldest – then take the small road to your right opposite the second station exit.

4 TAKESHITA-DORI

Takeshita-dori is crammed with Tokyo's pampered teenagers, buying jeans and T-shirts, eating hamburgers or just hanging out.

Turn right at the end of Takeshita-dori and walk along Meiji-dori to the main intersection. Turn right here and right again for Ota Art Museum (see page 38) or left on to Omotesando to continue the walk.

5 OMOTESANDO

Omotesando is the epitome of chic Tokyo, and becomes more chic the further you proceed. Nicknamed the Japanese Champs Élysées, this broad, tree-lined boulevard was built at the time of the Tokyo Olympics in 1964. Its glossy stores house expensive boutiques and elegant street cafés where you can sit and watch the

passing crowd. On the right, look for the Oriental Bazaar (see page 152), and the elegant Hanae Mori Building, showcase for Hanae Mori, doyenne of Tokyo fashion designers.

The tour ends at Omotesando subway station, at the top of the street. If you're feeling energetic, carry on straight across the traffic lights into the Aoyama area, where Tokyo's world-famous fashion designers – Issey Miyake, Comme des Garçons and Yohji Yamamoto – have boutiques. At the end of the road is one of Tokyo's best museums, the Nezu Art Museum (see page 37).

Shibuya is a magnet for youth – and a great area to see and be seen

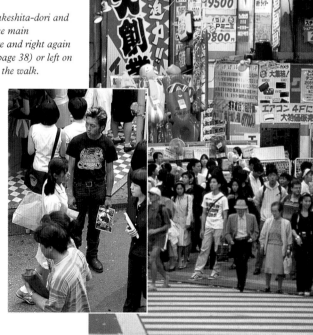

Hot Springs

For sheer sybaritic pleasure, there is little to beat the Japanese hot-spring experience. After a hard day's travelling you arrive at your inn, late in the afternoon. You put on the *yukata* (dressing gown) provided and immediately head for the bath. These days there are usually separate baths for men and women, though sometimes the baths are mixed. You scrub yourself well outside the tub, rinse off and finally – with a blissful sigh – ease gently into the steaming water. Japanese baths are usually scalding hot, but get in, sit very still and let the heat of the water ease away your tension and tiredness.

The land of Japan is like the lid of a pressure cooker, sitting on a cauldron of volcanic activity. As a result hot water, laden with healthful minerals, bursts out of the earth all over the country. Different waters are said to be good for different ailments. The water at Atami (see page 40) contains calcium sulphate and is good for the nerves and skin, while the waters at Beppu (see page 132) contain a pot-pourri of minerals that will heal a

Taking the waters has always been one of Japan's great pleasures: Beppu's famous hot springs (bottom left); lava fields at Noboribetsu; outdoor hot spring; a detail from the Emperor's bath in Dogo Onsen

multitude of ailments – and give you beautiful skin to boot.

Japanese have been taking the waters as far back as memory stretches. Today there are more than 20,000 thermal spas. Besides simple hot tubs, you can bathe in an outdoor pool (*rotemburo*), with the stars twinkling overhead, or sit in a hot waterfall or in the mouth of a cave while the moon rises over the ocean, or be buried up to your neck in mineral-rich hot sand. In fact you will soon discover that the best way to get to know a region is to try out its hot springs.

Kamakura

*T*he ancient city of Kamakura has temples, shrines, beautiful gardens, hills good for hiking and even a beach. Many people choose to live in these peaceful hills rather than in Tokyo: the city has become famous as the home of scholars, writers and artists. It is also one of Tokyo's most popular seaside resorts, though in summer the beach is barely visible beneath all the people.

Kamakura's heyday lasted for 140 years, from 1192 to 1333. The first shogun, Yoritomo Minamoto made it his capital. Here he and his successors, tough military men, had their court. Under their patronage many temples were built and beautiful images carved. Then in 1333, after bitter fighting, they were defeated by a rival clan. Power reverted to Kyoto, and Kamakura became a sleepy fishing town, full of monuments to its past grandeur.

HASE-DERA TEMPLE

The grounds of this ancient temple are littered with images of Jizo, the Bodhisattva (divine being) responsible for children. Mothers who have miscarried or had abortions clothe the small statues with bibs. But the glory of the temple is its towering 9m camphor-wood statue of Kannon, deity of mercy. Legend has it that it was carved in the Nara area, then cast into the sea to find its divinely-appointed place. It drifted ashore at Kamakura in 736.

5 minutes' walk from Hase station. Open: 7am–5.40pm March to September, 7am–4.40pm in winter. Admission charge.

KOTOKUIN DAIBUTSU (Great Buddha)

The Great Buddha is the symbol of Kamakura. The seated figure is 11.4m tall – as big as a small house – and towers above the surrounding trees. Cast in bronze in 1252, the Buddha sits, his eyes cast down in meditation, emanating peace and serenity. The temple which once housed the image was washed away by a tidal wave in 1495, and ever since the Buddha has sat out in the open.

10 minutes' walk from Hase station. Open: 7am–6.30pm June to August, 7am–6pm April to May and September to October, 7am–5.30pm in winter. Admission charge.

TSURUGAOKA HACHIMAN-GU (Hachiman Shrine)

The shrine to Hachiman, god of war, is the heart of Kamakura. Leave the station and you come almost immediately to a broad avenue crossed by huge *torii* (gates). This is Wakamiya Oji (Avenue of the Young Prince), which leads from the beach all the way to Hachiman Shrine.

Founded in 1063, the shrine was moved to its present position on Tsurugaoka (Crane Hill) by Shogun Yoritomo in 1191. As you approach it, you come to Drum Bridge, as steep as the side of a drum, which only the shogun was allowed to cross. The shrine itself, a splendid vermilion structure, is at the top of a long flight of steps; if you look back from here you see the sea behind you.

Hachiman is always bustling with people. Not to be missed is the archery contest on 16 September, when mounted archers in medieval costume, galloping at full pelt, send arrows winging to hit three small targets.

Kamakura's spectacular Great Buddha keeps watch over the city

10 minutes' walk from Kamakura station. Always open; admission free.

ZENIARAI BENTEN

Enclosed within a natural cavern, surrounded by moss and dangling tree roots, this atmospheric old shrine is full of ponds, small shrines, altars, fortune-tellers and incense smoke. Its enormous popularity is due to the miraculous properties of its water. It is said that if you wash your money here, it will double in value: you put your cash in the wicker baskets provided, then dry the notes in the incense smoke.

25 minutes' walk west of Kamakura station. Always open; admission free.

Kamakura is 1 hour south of Tokyo by train. See also pages 56–7.

A splendid old heavy-walled house, fitted with fireproof shutters, in Kawagoe

KAWAGOE

This small castle town still retains something of the flavour of old Edo (pre-modern Tokyo). After a disastrous fire in 1893, many fireproof storehouses and shops were built with thick walls of clay and plaster, tiny shuttered windows and steep tiled roofs. Several of these handsome black buildings line the main shopping street. Don't miss Kita-en Temple, the birthplace of Shogun Ieyasu Tokugawa.

50 minutes' northwest of Tokyo by train. Kita-en, 10 minutes' walk from Hon-Kawagoe station. Open: daily, 9am–4.30pm April to November, 9am–4pm in winter. Admission charge.

MIURA

Beyond Kamakura is the Miura Peninsula, one of the nearest areas of countryside to Tokyo. Off the main roads there is good walking, beaches, old temples and picturesque fishing villages. Miura is particularly associated with the British navigator Will Adams, whose life inspired the novel and film *Shogun*. Blown off course, Adams dropped anchor in Japan in 1600. He struck up a friendship with the shogun Ieyasu Tokugawa and taught the Japanese the art of shipbuilding.

1½ hours south of Tokyo by rail and road.

NARITA

Long before Japan's international airport opened at Narita, pilgrims were coming to worship at Shinshoji. Set in cedar groves rising out of the rice fields, this splendid old temple was founded in 939; most of the present buildings, including the beautiful three-storey pagoda, date from the last century. The main image, the fierce deity Fudo Myoo, is very ancient and was brought from Kyoto around 940.

1 hour east of Tokyo by train; 20 minutes by bus from Narita airport. Shinshoji: 15 minutes' walk from Narita station, through the Omotesando shopping district.

O-SHIMA ISLAND

Scattered south of Tokyo are seven islands, an extension of the Fuji-Hakone volcanic chain. At the centre of the largest, O-shima, is Mount Mihara, which erupted spectacularly in 1986 for several months. Today it is placid and O-shima has regained its status as Tokyo's nearest tropical paradise. There is a wonderful outdoor hot spring on Mount Mihara, in a cave overhung with vines and creepers, and the mountaintop affords fine views of Mount Fuji and the seven islands. O-shima is known as Camellia Island for its beautiful camellia bushes, which produce an oil used to gloss sumo wrestlers' hair.

Accessible by plane and ferry.

YOKOHAMA

Yokohama is a lively city famous for its international flavour. The arrival of the first western ships 150 years ago turned it into the country's most important port. Westerners were encouraged to settle here, at a safe distance from Tokyo, and there is still a large western community along with a thriving cricket club. Yokohama is now Japan's second largest city and a vital commercial and industrial hub.

The city itself is very pleasant. It has the largest Chinatown in Japan, and people come here to imbibe the exotic atmosphere and dine on the country's best Chinese food. On the southeast edge of the city is Sankei-en Garden, laid out by Tomitaro Hara, a millionaire silk merchant, in 1906. Scattered around the beautifully landscaped grounds are villas, tea pavilions, farmhouses and a 500-year-old pagoda that were brought here from all over Japan.

Yokohama's profile is changing rapidly. There is a splendid new Bay Bridge across the harbour, glittering at night, which you can admire from the soaring skyscrapers that make up the futuristic Minato-mirai development.

30 minutes south of Tokyo by train; also accessible by plane, ship and road. Chinatown: at Ishikawa-cho station. Sankei-en, 10 minutes' walk from Yamate station. Open: daily, outer garden 9am–4.30pm, inner garden 9am–4pm. Admission charge.

Yokohama's lively Chinatown has the best Chinese food in the country

Climbing Mount Fuji

Everyone wants to climb Fuji once – though, as the Japanese proverb goes, only a fool would climb it twice. The official climbing season is July and August. During this period, buses run straight from Tokyo to the fifth station (call Fuji Kyuko, tel: 03 3374 2221, to book), and the mountain huts along the path are open.

Fuji is a real mountain. Be prepared for cold and sudden changes in weather; even at the height of summer it is freezing cold and very windy at the top. It is also high enough, at 3,776m, to produce mild altitude sickness. You will need a sweater, rainwear, hat and gloves, hiking boots, a torch and a staff. *Allow 2 days and 1 night.*

Climb begins at the fifth station. Out of season, take train or bus to Lake Kawaguchi (Kawaguchi-ko).

1 KAWAGUCHI-KO (Lake Kawaguchi)
On a fine day you can see Fuji, very close, gloriously reflected in the lake.
Buses leave hourly for the 50-minute journey to the 5th station.

2 GO-GOME (Fifth Station)
Many people go to the fifth station for a day trip. From here, halfway up Fuji, you can stroll in either direction along a broad, level path with, on fine days, wonderful views across the surrounding country.
The climbing path is well marked.

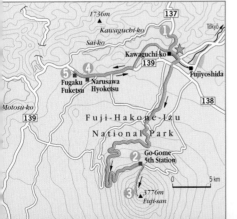

3 THE SUMMIT
The path starts off steep and gets ever steeper. From the sixth station you are above the tree line, walking on dusty volcanic gravel. The climb from the seventh to the ninth stations is the hardest. At each station there are huts where you can buy a bowl of noodles, and also a *torii* and a shrine – for the

Beautiful as it is, Fuji is a real mountain, so 'Keep to the footpath', as the sign says!

Japanese, this is a pilgrimage as well as a hike. If you want to see the sunrise, rest at the seventh or eighth stations and complete your climb just before dawn.

Arriving at the summit is a truly exhilarating experience. There is a *torii* across the path and a shrine at the top, where a Shinto priest conducts a dawn ceremony. There is also – this being Japan – a sizeable souvenir shop. With luck the sunrise will be breathtakingly beautiful, pale lemon spreading across the sky with clouds rolling below you. As the sun rises, watch for the huge shadow of Fuji spread across the clouds. It takes an hour to walk around the crater (the highest point is marked by the weather station on the far side).
Return the way you came, or take the Sunabashiri route, sliding on volcanic gravel, back to the fifth station in 2½–3hours. From here return to Tokyo; or take a bus to Narusawa cave, via Lake Kawaguchi.

4 NARUSAWA HYOKETSU (Narusawa Ice Cave)

Near Fuji there are two caves formed by pockets of gas trapped in the lava during an eruption thousands of years ago. Narusawa Ice Cave is icy-cold, even at the height of summer.
Take the hiking trail through the woods to Fugaku Wind Cave.

5 FUGAKU FUKETSU (Fugaku Wind Cave)

Fugaku Wind Cave is a series of caverns, with fantastically shaped stalagmites.
From here take a bus back to Lake Kawaguchi and thence to Tokyo.

The Mt Fuji English Climbing Info telephone/fax service is supplied free of charge by Fuji Yoshida Tourist Information Office. Tel: 0555 22 9070; fax: 0555 22 0703.

Hakone

This circuit of the lovely Hakone region by mountain railway, funicular railway, cable car and boat, can be done as a day trip from Tokyo; or stop over at a hot spring inn. On a fine day there are wonderful views of Fuji. *Day trip.*

At the Odakyu line station in Shinjuku, buy a 'free pass' which gives you unlimited travel in Hakone on most transport for four days. Take the train to Odawara.

1 ODAWARA

Odawara was once an important castle town. The present castle is a 1960 reconstruction of the 1416 original.
At Odawara station, board the Hakone-Tozan mountain railway, which toils slowly up the wooded hillside. Alight at Miyanoshita. Turn left out of the station and stroll up the hill through the village.

2 MIYANOSHITA

Miyanoshita is a famous Japanese spa and home to the glorious old Fujiya Hotel. Built in 1878, the Fujiya is reminiscent of the Raffles in Singapore; everyone from Charlie Chaplin to Albert Einstein has stayed there.
Take the Hakone-Tozan railway on to Chokoku-no-mori.

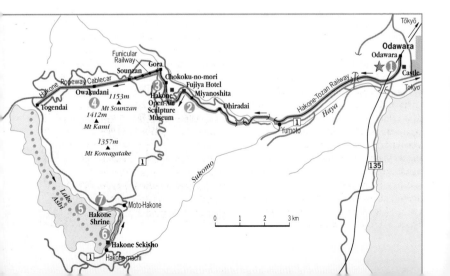

3 CHOKOKU-NO-MORI (Hakone Open-air Sculpture Museum)

Spread across the open hillside is a collection of modern sculptures by western and Japanese artists, including one of the world's largest collections of works by British sculptor Henry Moore. There is also a museum devoted to Pablo Picasso's ceramics.

Take the Hakone-Tozan railway on to the terminus, Gora. Change there for the funicular railway which takes you to Sounzan Station. From there take the Hakone Ropeway cable car.

4 OWAKUDANI

The cable car swings high above a spectacular volcanic landscape, with glorious views of Fuji, filling half the horizon. Halfway across, alight at Owakudani ('great boiling valley'), from where you can stroll between boiling mud pools and vents of sulphurous steam and buy a naturally boiled egg.

Take the cable car on to the terminus, Togendai.

5 LAKE ASHI

At Togendai, a Spanish galleon is waiting to sail you across Lake Ashi, the heart of Hakone. On fine days Mount Fuji soars above this lovely lake, perfectly mirrored in its waters. There are hotels, watersports and fine hiking here. To your left, as you near the town of Hakone, watch for the red *torii* of Hakone Shrine, standing in the water.

Alight at Hakone-machi (Hakone town) and walk left from the port through the village to Hakone checkpoint.

The best way to enjoy the full splendour of Lake Ashi is from the cable car

6 HAKONE SEKISHO (Hakone Checkpoint)

In the days of the shoguns, all travellers on the main road between Edo (old Tokyo) and Kyoto had to stop at this police checkpoint, where they were thoroughly searched. The museum contains weapons and photographs of criminals' severed heads, stuck on poles.

Take the footpath lined with cedars along the edge of the lake to Hakone Shrine, just beyond Moto-Hakone village. There are also buses.

7 HAKONE SHRINE

This beautiful old shrine, founded in 757, stands in a grove of ancient cryptomeria trees. From the shrine follow the cobbled steps down to the lakeside, where the large red *torii* stands in the water.

From Moto-Hakone take a bus back to Odawara, from where there are frequent trains back to Tokyo.

> **Chokoku-no-mori** – 3 minutes' walk from Chokoku-no-mori station. Tel: 0460 2 1161. Open: daily, 9am–5pm March to October, 9am–4pm in winter. Admission charge.
> **Hakone Sekisho museum** – Open: daily, 9am–4.30pm (until 4pm in winter). Admission charge.

Kita-Kamakura and Kamakura

This walk takes you from the serene Zen temples of Kita-Kamakura (North Kamakura), along a trail through the hills above the city, to Kamakura's celebrated Hachiman Shrine.
Allow 4 hours.

Kita-Kamakura is 55 minutes south of Tokyo by train. Engakuji is just outside the station.

1 ENGAKUJI

Many lay people come to this famous Zen temple, founded in 1282, to learn Zen meditation. The path to the left of the main hall leads via the relic hall and a thatched sub-temple, where you can have green tea, to an attractive garden enclosed by hills. The path to the right leads to the temple's Great Bell, cast in 1301.
Return to the road and follow the tracks to a level crossing. Turn left along the main road to the huge gate of Kenchoji

2 KENCHOJI

This is the most important of Kamakura's Zen temples. Pass the Great Gate and the atmospheric old Buddha Hall, which houses a statue of Jizo, the Bodhisattva who protects children. Don't miss the fine Zen garden behind the Dragon Hall, with a pond shaped like the character for 'heart'. Follow the path on and up to a *torii* and two stone lions, marking the entrance to Hansobo. Climb up to this strange little shrine, past more stone lions and metal images of 'mountain goblins' – winged and beaked mountain priests.
Take the stone steps up on to the hill. There is a clear hiking trail along the ridge, through woods and bamboo groves. After 30 minutes, you come to a large signpost where two paths cross. Take the right-hand path down to a road. Kakuonji is 250m up the road to your right.

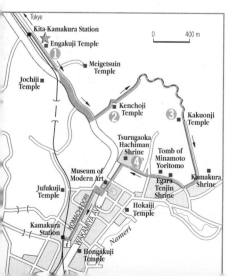

Engakuji – Open: daily, 8am–4pm
(until 5pm in summer). Admission
charge.
Kenchoji – Tel: 0467 22 0981. Open:
daily, 9am–4.30pm. Admission
charge.
Kakuonji – Open: daily for tours at
10am, 11am, 1pm, 2pm and 3pm,
except on rainy days; closed in
August. Admission charge.

3 KAKUONJI

Much loved by Kamakura residents,
Kakuonji is a peaceful retreat, tucked
away at the end of a long valley. If you
arrive on the hour on a fine day (except
August), one of the monks will show
you the temple's wonderful Buddha
images and the Black Jizo, said to be
blackened from rescuing sinners from
hell.
*Return down the road to Kamakura Shrine
(1869). Follow the road to your right,
which leads from the front of the shrine, to
another road, signposted in English 'Egara
Tenjin Shrine'. This small back street leads
to Hachiman Shrine.*

4 TSURUGAOKA HACHIMAN-GU (Hachiman Shrine)

Along the way, you can drop in to Egara
Tenjin Shrine, dedicated to the god of
scholarship. You also pass the
surprisingly humble tomb of the first
shogun, Yoritomo Minamoto. At a
T junction, turn left, then right, and you
will find yourself walking along the
avenue used for horseback archery every
16 September. After exploring
Hachiman (see page 48), you can stroll
down the broad avenue which leads
from the front of the shrine, built by
Shogun Yoritomo in 1182. At cherry

Hachiman Shrine is the ancient heart of
Kamakura and a popular place of worship

blossom time this is particularly
beautiful. Or turn right from the shrine
entrance, then left down Komachi-dori
(Komachi Street), full of restaurants,
teahouses, souvenir shops and shops
selling *Kamakura-bori*, the lacquerware
for which Kamakura is famous.
*Either way, you will end up at Kamakura
station, from where there are frequent trains
back to Tokyo.*

PAINTING, POTTERY

Japanese artists have always loved and celebrated their own country and its landscape. One of the most famous is the woodblock-print master Katsushika Hokusai (1760–1849). His celebrated *Thirty-six Views of Mount Fuji* show Fuji under rain, at sunset, through the arch of a bridge or across a temple roof. His younger and equally famous rival was Ando Hiroshige (1797–1858), whose *Fifty-three Stations of the Tokaido* is a series of wonderfully vivid scenes showing each town along the Tokaido, the famous road between Edo (old Tokyo) and Kyoto.

Artists of earlier eras too often painted landscapes, in which buildings and people are but a tiny part of the whole scene. The great master of monochrome ink painting was Sesshu (1420–1506), who created a universe with a few brushstrokes, using nothing but black ink.

In Japan pottery is a fine art and master potters are among the country's most revered artists. Throughout Japan are pottery towns: Imbe *(Bizen* ware – see page 122), Hagi (*Hagi-yaki* rose-coloured pottery – see page 121) and Iga Ueno (*Iga-yaki* stoneware – see page 98) are among the most famous. The pottery of each area is distinguished by the quality of the local clay and the wood used in firing, as well as by the potters' style.

AND THE NOVEL

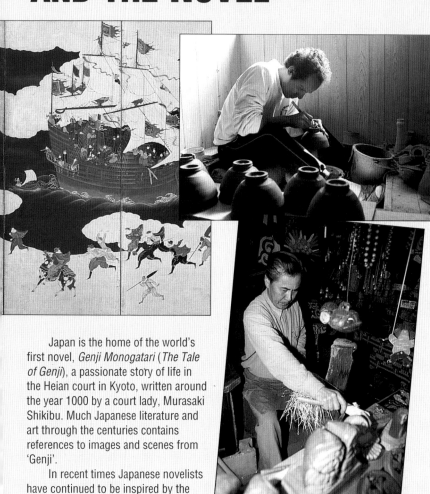

Japan is the home of the world's first novel, *Genji Monogatari* (*The Tale of Genji*), a passionate story of life in the Heian court in Kyoto, written around the year 1000 by a court lady, Murasaki Shikibu. Much Japanese literature and art through the centuries contains references to images and scenes from 'Genji'.

In recent times Japanese novelists have continued to be inspired by the beauty of the Japanese landscape. Nobel-prize winner Yasunari Kawabata (1899–1972) set his most famous work, *Snow Country*, in the romantic snow-bound country of the Japan Sea coast. Another of his popular works is *The Izu Dancer*, set in the Izu peninsula.

An exquisite gold Muromachi screen painting showing the arrival of the first foreigners to Japan; a Hagi potter at work; and an Ainu woodcarving in Hokkaido

The North

*T*he north is a region of magnificent unspoilt scenery, with primeval land-scapes created by volcanic eruptions and sweeping vistas of lakes, mountains and forests. Visitors come here to enjoy nature rather than the works of man: there are few temples, castles and monuments to traditional Japanese culture.

This is traditionally the poorest, most underprivileged part of the country. Both Tohoku – the northern part of Honshu – and Hokkaido were originally the home of non-Japanese peoples, who were gradually driven northwards by the Japanese. Colonisation of Hokkaido in fact began as recently as 1868, and here you can still see remnants of the culture of the island's original inhabitants, the Ainu (see pages 66–7).

The region is largely agricultural. Country life goes on much as it did hundreds of years ago, and there is much of old Japan here. Recently, as the Japanese have discovered leisure, it has also become a prime holiday area. In winter people come to ski, in summer to walk or play golf.

The greatest walker of all was the 17th-century poet Matsuo Basho (see page 96), who roamed Tohoku 300 years ago and wrote a travel diary, *The Narrow Road to the Deep North*. Throughout the north are places he immortalised in his exquisite poems.

AKAN NATIONAL PARK

The three mysterious caldera lakes of Akan – Lake Akan itself, mysterious Lake Mashu and Lake Kussharo, said to be the home of a monster – have some of the most breathtaking scenery in Hokkaido. There is a small, brand-new Ainu museum on the shores of Lake Kussharo. (See also page 144.)
Hokkaido. Approach by bus or rented car from Bihoro, 5 hours by train east of Sapporo.

DAISETSUZAN NATIONAL PARK

Daisetsuzan's beauties lie at two levels. Below, accessible by car, is Sounkyo Gorge with its ravines and vertiginous cliff faces, one of Hokkaido's most famous sights. Above, the domain of hikers and skiers, are the spectacular peaks, a landscape of dark, cinder-sloped volcanic cones and craters, where icy winds blow even at the height of summer and steam gushes from the ground. There is an Ainu museum in the town of Asahikawa, on the far side of the park,

THE YAMABUSHI

The wandering ascetic priests called *yamabushi* are the guardians of the sacred mountains. In the past they could be found all over Japan, clad in their distinctive garb of black pillbox hat, checked blouse and deerskin leggings, and carrying a huge conch shell which they blew like a horn. They practised the esoteric Shugendo religion, a form of Tantric Buddhism, and often performed the role of sorcerers and exorcists. Nowadays many apparent *yamabushi* turn out to be farmers or businessmen taking a few days off, though you can still find full-time *yamabushi* leading pilgrims across the three sacred mountains.

The stern beauty of Daisetsuzan National Park, with its lush gorges, rocks and waterfalls

where you can see Ainu dances. (See also page 144.)

Hokkaido. Approach from Asahikawa or Kamikawa, 1½–2 hours northeast of Sapporo by train, then by bus or rented car.

DEWA SANZAN (Three Mountains of Dewa)

The three mountains of Dewa (the old name for northeast Tohoku) are among the most sacred in Japan, strewn with temples and small stone shrines. Japanese come from all over the country on pilgrimage, and even the least religious cannot fail to feel the power of the place. Holiest is Mount Yudono, home of a deity who resides in a hot spring. Near by are two temples with the remains of monks who literally mummified themselves in order to become Buddhas before their deaths. (See also page 146.)

Tohoku. 1½ hours by bus northwest of Yamagata; accessible by plane or train (2 hours) from Tokyo.

THE NORTH

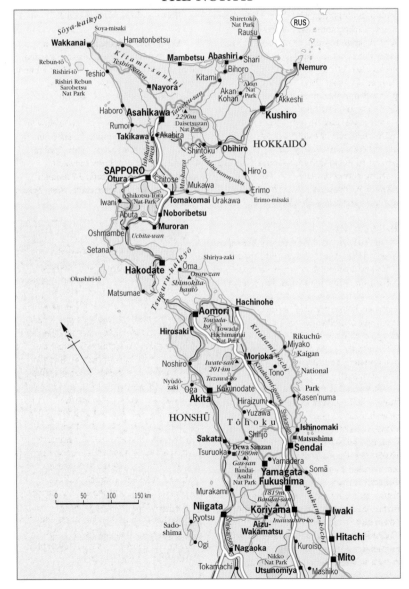

HAKODATE

For centuries the Japanese toehold on Hokkaido was the port city of Hakodate, at its southernmost tip. When the west forced Japan to open to trade in 1854, Hakodate was one of the first treaty ports, and the city still retains its historic flavour. Goryaku Fort, with its five-pointed star-shaped grounds, is Japan's first western-style fort. Take the cable car up Mount Hakodate for a spectacular night view over the city; stroll the streets of the old town, Motomachi, full of well-preserved Meiji-period buildings; or take a cruise across the bay.

Hokkaido. 4 hours south of Sapporo by train; also accessible by plane.

HIRAIZUMI

In his *Travels*, the 15th-century Venetian, Marco Polo, wrote of a country called 'Zipangu', where the palaces were of solid gold. The city he was describing was Hiraizumi. For a hundred years, between 1089 and 1189, Hiraizumi was the heart of a vibrant culture, based on the gold which was mined in the region. Although the great city has long since disappeared, enough remains to suggest what it was like.

One small temple completely covered in gold leaf still remains – the Konjikido (Golden Hall), part of Chusonji. Covered in fabulous ornamentation, the Golden Hall houses a statue of Amida, Buddha of the Western Paradise, surrounded by attendants. Buried beneath the three altars are the three Fujiwara lords who ruled Hiraizumi during its heyday. Chusonji itself is a complex of many temples, stretching up a hillside through groves of ancient cryptomeria trees. The poet Basho visited in 1689 and wrote one of his most famous *haiku*:

'Summer grasses
– the aftermath
of ancient warriors' dreams!'

Also worth visiting is Motsuji, a temple that was once a pleasure garden of princes and nobles, where they whiled away their days composing verses, paddling languidly in boats and sipping *sake*.

Tohoku. About 3 hours north of Tokyo by train. Chusonji, 20 minutes' walk from station. Open: daily, 8am–5pm April to October, 8.30am–4.30pm in winter. Admission charge. Motsuji, 10 minutes' walk from station. Open: daily, 8am–5pm. Admission charge.

YOSHITSUNE

The epic *Tale of the Heike* and numerous *kabuki* and *noh* dramas celebrate the exploits of Japan's great medieval hero, Minamoto no Yoshitsune. When Yoshitsune was born in 1159, two warrior clans – the Taira and Minamoto – were battling to rule Japan. He led the Minamoto to victory, but his elder brother, Shogun Yoritomo, was jealous of his success and demanded his head.

Accompanied by a few faithful retainers, Yoshitsune fled north and in 1189 took refuge in the independent kingdom of Hiraizumi. His trust was misplaced. The ruler, the treacherous Yasuhira, surrounded Yoshitsune's castle, where the hero's retainers defended him just long enough for him to commit honourable suicide.

Yasuhira's treachery did not pay off. The shogun attacked the northern kingdom and the great civilisation of Hiraizumi came to an end.

Matsushima is justly considered to be one of the three most beautiful places in Japan

KAKUNODATE

Kakunodate is famous for its streets of lovely old samurai houses, lined with dark wooden fences overhung with luxuriant weeping cherry trees. The town was carefully planned at the beginning of the Tokugawa shogunate era, around 1620, with two completely separate areas – one for merchants, one for samurai – divided by an open plaza which acted as a firebreak. The merchant quarter has grown into a modern commercial centre, but much of the samurai district is lovingly preserved. Some of the poorer samurai made a living by making cups, vases and tea ceremony caddies covered in polished cherry bark; many shops in the area specialise in this attractive handicraft.

Tohoku. 45 minutes west of Morioka by train. Samurai houses open: daily, 9am–5pm April to November, 9am–4.30pm in winter. Admission charge for some, others free.

MASHIKO

Pottery lovers will enjoy a visit to Mashiko, a small pleasant country town put on the map when one of Japan's most famous potters, Shoji Hamada (1894–1978), set up his kiln here in 1924. It is now home to dozens of potters, and young people from all over the world come here to learn the art of Japanese pottery.

Karito. 2 hours north of Tokyo by train and bus (change at Utsunomiya).

HIROSAKI

This charming northern city preserves much of the flavour of the past. It was formerly the capital of the Tsugaru clan, who ruled over the rugged northernmost province of Honshu. It has two sights well worth stopping for, both oases of tranquillity. The 17th-century temple, Choshoji, with its massive triple-storey front gate, is flanked by an avenue of 33 temples, lined with pine trees. Hirosaki Castle, one of the few genuinely old castles remaining in Japan, stands on a bluff above the town, in a pleasant park and surrounded by three moats covered in water-lilies.

Tohoku. About 4 hours by road or rail northwest of Morioka.

MATSUSHIMA

When the poet Basho visited Matsushima Bay in 1689, he was so overcome by its beauty that he could not write a single word. Matsushima – the name means 'pine islands' – is still

exquisitely beautiful, tiny craggy islets crowned with gnarled pines, set in a jewel-blue sea. You can stroll the shoreline, studded with islands and temples, including the ancient Zen temple of Zuiganji, or take a boat around the outlying islands. You will, however, share your enjoyment with thousands of others. Matsushima is one of the three most celebrated views in Japan, a popular holiday and honeymoon spot, full of people and hotels. For those in search of peace and quiet, the tranquil paddy fields and hills of nearby Oku Matsushima and the island of Kinkazan, home to deer and monkeys, are a better bet.
Tohoku. 1 hour north of Sendai by train.

MORIOKA
Once the castle town of the lords of Nambu, Morioka is a large pleasant city, surrounded by densely forested hills.

Nothing remains of the castle except the moat and some ruinous walls, but across the river is an attractive artisans' area with many old shops, housing dyers, metal workers and bakers of *sembei* (rice crackers). On Mount Iwate, with a fine view across the city, is an eccentric and wonderful museum created by a local 19th-century artist, Yaoji Hashimoto. It rambles through several ancient and beautifully renovated farmhouses, and includes fine examples of local ironware, pottery and handicrafts as well as the artist's own paintings.
Tohoku. 2½–3½ hours north of Tokyo by train. Morioka Hashimoto Bijutsukan (Morioka Hashimoto Museum of Art), 30 minutes by bus from station. Tel: 0196 52 5002. Open: daily 10am–5pm. Admission charge.

A cave in Matsushima where monks would once retreat for meditation

THE AINU

Dotted around the lakesides and plains of Hokkaido are totem poles, small houses with thatched roofs and souvenir stalls selling wooden carvings, vestiges of a near-vanished culture.

Hokkaido and northeastern Honshu were formerly the domain of a variety of tribes known as the Ainu. Racially they are distinct from the Japanese, with lighter skin, a heavier brow ridge and deep-set eyes, sometimes grey or blue. The men are distinguished by their luxuriant head hair, beards and moustaches.

The Ainu once lived by hunting, fishing and gathering plants. They made bows and arrows, carved canoes from tree trunks, and wore robes of elm-bark or cotton, appliquéd with distinctive geometric whorls. When the women married they tattooed around their mouths.

They had a rich oral culture, epic poems passed from generation to generation. They worshipped the spirits of animals and plants, especially the bear, owl and sea turtle. Once a year they performed the Iomante ceremony, a form of fertility festival in which a bear was sacrificed and its spirit sent heavenward.

For centuries the Ainu were driven further and further north, and after the Japanese colonised Hokkaido in 1868 they became second-class citizens. Today, after a century of intermarriage, there are only 25,000 full-blooded Ainu left, plus another 25,000 who are part Japanese. The Ainu language has nearly died out with

few young people able to speak it, but in recent years the younger Ainu have begun to take a pride in their ancestral heritage. There is a growing Ainu movement and in August 1994 a leading Ainu activist won a seat in the Upper House of the Japanese Diet.

Visitors can get a glimpse of this disappearing Ainu world in a few museums and rather sad Ainu villages,

Relics of a vanishing way of life: an Ainu village in Hokkaido; an Ainu craftsman at work on a woodcarving; intricate embroidery on a traditional Ainu costume; and a re-created family scene around the hearth

where customs and handicrafts are preserved and impoverished Ainu elders conduct their ancient ceremonies, rituals and dances.

Nikko

*N*o emperor ever had a monument as overwhelmingly lavish as the shogun's tomb at Nikko. After Ieyasu Tokugawa's death, his grandson Iemitsu planned a mausoleum that would demonstrate the shogunate's incredible wealth and power. To finance it, he took 'donations' from the *daimyo*, thus ensuring that none would ever be able to finance a rebellion. The Toshogu Shrine took two years to complete, starting in 1634. An army of 15,000 artisans worked on it; 38 tonnes of red lacquer and 2.5 million sheets of gold leaf coated its walls.

The ornate buildings are in a spectacular mountain setting, surrounded by ancient cryptomeria forests. Nearby are Lake Chuzenji, which on a clear day reflects the volcanic cone of Mount Nantai in its waters, and the mighty Kegon Falls.

Nikko is one of Japan's most popular destinations. Try to visit early or late to avoid the crowds. Before entering the shrines, buy a strip of tickets allowing entry into the four main sights (paying separately for each costs far more).

Rinnoji

Rinnoji dates from 766; the present magnificent buildings were rebuilt as part of Iemitsu's grand plan. The main hall houses three massive gilt Buddhist images.

Shinkyo Bridge

This beautiful old bridge of faded red and gold marks the approach to the shrines. In the past only shoguns and imperial envoys could cross.

Taiyuin-byo

The last complex you come to, set against the mountain, is the mausoleum of Iemitsu Tokugawa. In structure it is a smaller version of the Toshogu Shrine, but different in style, less ornate, more unified and sophisticated. Brilliantly painted green and red deities stand against a background of peonies. Look for the Kokamon beside the main shrine, said to resemble the gate of the legendary Dragon King's palace under the sea.

Toshogu Shrine

The Toshogu Shrine is a far cry from the Zen restraint which westerners associate with Japanese aesthetics. Every possible surface is covered in ornamentation: animals, sages, gods and birds peep from every frieze and cornice. The buildings

---

IEYASU TOKUGAWA (1543–1616)

More than anyone else, Ieyasu Tokugawa changed the course of Japanese history. In the mid-16th century, Japan was racked by civil war as one warlord after another strove to expand his domains and take over the country. Ieyasu, who has become proverbial for his patience, simply waited until eventually, in 1600, he defeated the last of his enemies. He became shogun and instituted the system which was to keep the country at peace, and under the control of the Tokugawa family, for the next 250 years. After his death, he was interred at Nikko; the Toshogu Shrine was later built as his mausoleum.

are arranged on a series of levels, and gates – each more splendid than the last – lead ever deeper into the heart of the shrine.

In the first enclosure, look for the relief of two elephants, carved by an artist who had clearly never seen one, and the three wise monkeys, an emblem of Nikko. The most dazzling and famous structure is the Yomeimon, nicknamed the Twilight Gate because you could spend all day from dawn to dusk looking at it. One of the pillars is carved upside down, to stop the gods being jealous of such perfection. Lower-ranking samurai could not pass this gate. Beyond is the main shrine, dedicated to Ieyasu, and – at the top of 207 steps – the small tomb containing his ashes.

Nikko shrines and temples open: daily, 8am–5pm April to October, 8am–4pm in winter. Admission charge

Nikko is 2 hours north of Tokyo by train. Tourist information office at station.

'Never say *kekko* (splendid) until you've seen Nikko' goes the saying. The three wise monkeys (Hear No Evil, Speak No Evil, See No Evil) are its symbol

NOBORIBETSU

The pungent smell of sulphur and steam seeping from every drain and crevice greet you in Noboribetsu, Hokkaido's most famous spa. For those partial to hot spring bathing, the Dai-ichi Takimoto-kan has over 40 different sorts of baths. You can visit the Ainu village, or Jigoku-dani (Hell Valley) behind the town, where mud pools boil and sputter and steam jets into the air.

Hokkaido. 1 hour by train south of Sapporo, then 15 minutes by bus to the spa.

OSORE-ZAN (Mount Osore)

Osore-zan, in the far northeast of Honshu, is one of the weirdest places on earth and worth the enormous difficulty of getting there. The time to see this unearthly volcanic landscape is in July, when people come from as far as Tokyo to consult blind mediums in the temple on the edge of the crater lake. (See also page 147.)

Tohoku. 35 minutes by infrequent bus from Mutsu, 2 hours by train north of Aomori. Aomori is accessible by plane, or 5 hours north of Tokyo by train.

SADO-SHIMA (Sado Island)

Those in search of peace and quiet could do worse than visit sleepy, unspoilt Sado, off Honshu's northwest coast, where terraced paddy fields glint in the sun amid forested hills. The fifth largest of Japan's islands, Sado was traditionally a place of exile for revolutionaries. After 1601, when gold was found at Aikawa in the remote northwest, criminals were sent to toil in the mines. Ferries arrive at Ryotsu, the main port, and from there you can explore the island by bus or rented car. You can tour the mines, or take the road along the north coast, winding along the clifftops to weather-beaten little fishing villages. Sado is famous for its unique puppet theatre, a primitive and wilder form of *bunraku* (see page 157). It is also home to the Kodo Drummers, whose exciting rhythms have become known world wide.

3 hours north of Tokyo by train and ferry, via Niigata, or by plane. Tourist information at Ryotsu ferry terminal.

SAPPORO

The capital and cultural centre of Hokkaido, Sapporo is a spacious, gracious city with leafy boulevards and a nightlife area, Susukino, claimed by the locals to be the liveliest north of Tokyo. Among the hotels and department stores are Meiji-period brick and timber-frame buildings. The Clock Tower, the city's symbol, dates from 1878. Don't miss the Batchelor Museum, a collection of 20,000 Ainu artefacts assembled by Victorian clergyman Dr John Batchelor.

Hokkaido. 11 hours north of Tokyo by train via Morioka or 16 hours direct; also accessible by plane. Batchelor Museum, in Botanical Gardens. Tel: 011 251 8010. Open: 9am–4pm, May to October; closed Monday and in winter. Admission charge.

A washtub boat bobbing on the waters off the tranquil island of Sado

The serene caldera lake, Shikotsu, is ringed by volcanoes

SENDAI

The capital of the Tohoku region, Sendai is a brash, modern city, totally rebuilt after the war. Historically it is famous as the capital of Date Masamune, the powerful 17th-century warlord known as the 'one-eyed dragon', who dominated the north. You can see the massive stone walls of his castle, Aoba-jo, in Aobayama Park.

Tohoku. 2 hours north of Tokyo by train. Aoba-jo ruins, 20 minutes by bus and on foot west of station. Open: 9am–4.15pm; closed Monday. Admission charge.

SHIKOTSU-TOYA NATIONAL PARK

Lake Shikotsu and Lake Toya form the twin hearts of this beautiful national park, within easy reach of Sapporo. Here you can visit crater lakes, spas and active volcanoes and walk or climb amid glorious mountain scenery. (See also page 145.)

Hokkaido. Accessible by bus from Sapporo or Chitose airport; also by train from Sapporo or Chitose to Tomakomai, then taxi to Lake Shikotsu, or to Toya for Lake Toya.

SHIRETOKO PENINSULA

Shiretoko has rugged volcanic scenery, waterfalls of mineral-filled hot water where you can bathe in natural pools in the rocks, and the possibility of encountering a bear in the mountains (see page 145).
Hokkaido. A day's journey east of Sapporo, by express (change at Abashiri), slow train to Shari, then bus. Or rent a car at Abashiri.

TAZAWA-KO (Lake Tazawa))

The deepest caldera lake in Japan, surrounded by wooded hills, Lake Tazawa is a centre for watersports. It is set in the midst of beautiful countryside, with rugged mountains near by, haunted by hikers in summer and skiers in winter. You can stay in one of the rustic inns here, accessible only on foot, where you are lit by oil lamp and dine on wild foods freshly picked from the mountains.
Tohoku. 40 minutes by train from Morioka, very near Kakunodate. Buses to lake and spa from station.

TONO

The remote Tohoku villages which together make up Tono first sprang to fame in 1910, when a folklorist called Kunio Yanagida published a collection of strange, rather disturbing local legends, *Tono Monogatari*. These tales of malevolent water-sprites, demons and the outlandish ways of rural folk later appeared in English as *The Legends of Tono*, translated by Robert Morse. Ever since then, visitors have gone to Tono in search of rustic peace. It is still a peaceful backwater (though gradually becoming spoilt), and you can still find waterwheels and houses where people live under the same roof as their horses. The best way by far to explore the area is to rent a bicycle.
Tohoku. 1½ hours southeast of Morioka by train. Bicycle hire available near station.

TOWADA-KO (Lake Towada)

Tohoku's premier resort, Lake Towada is overrun with Japanese tourists in buses in summer. It is nevertheless very beautiful – a large ancient caldera lake, deep and translucent, surrounded by rolling forested mountains. A popular walk is along pretty Oirase Gorge, but this is again very much set up for tourists. Tucked away in the hills round about are many old hot-spring inns.
Tohoku. 3 hours from Aomori and 2 hours from Hirosaki by bus.

TSURUOKA

A small, sleepy rural town, full of old farmers and wooden shop fronts, Tsuruoka is one of the gateways to Dewa Sanzan's sacred mountains (see page 61). Wander the streets and visit Chido Hakubutsukan (Chido Museum), housed in the gracious old villa of the once-powerful Sakae family.
Tohoku. 4 hours northwest of Sendai by train; also accessible from Niigata and Akita. Chido Museum, near castle, 10 minutes by bus from station. Tel: 0235 22 1199. Open: daily, 9am–5pm. Admission charge.

WAKKANAI

The windswept port of Wakkanai on the northernmost tip of Hokkaido is the ferry terminal for boats to the islands of Rebun and Rishiri, both remote and unspoilt and ideal for hikers (see page 145).
Hokkaido. 7 hours by train north of Sapporo; or by plane. Daily ferries and flights on to Rishiri and Rebun.

YAMADERA

At Yamadera, as the name ('Mountain Temple') suggests, the entire mountain is a temple. Scattered spectacularly across the steep wooded mountainside are small

The poet Basho and a modern-day tourist at Yamadera Temple

temples (some precariously balanced on stilts), stone images, and caves once the retreat of hermits. You climb the stone steps in company with many Japanese, who bring the ashes of their loved ones here to ensure that they will go to heaven. Inspired by the noisy whirr of the cicada, the poet Basho wrote one of his best-loved *haiku* here:

> 'The quiet –
> shrilling into the rocks
> the cicada's cry'.

1 hour by train from Sendai or 15 minutes from Yamagata.

Central Japan

Central Japan is where the great dramas of Japanese history were played out; for over 1,000 years, this was the heart of the country. Today, though Central Japan's metropolis, Tokyo, is the capital and the commercial hub of modern Japan, the traditional Japan of monks and geishas, tea ceremony and cherry blossom lives on here.

CENTRAL JAPAN

Suzu-misaki · Suzu · Wajima · Niigata · Nagaoka · Kashiwazaki · Ojiya · Jōetsu · Tōkamachi · Noto-hantō · Nanao · Itoigawa · Arai · Yuzawa · Hakui · Himi · Toyama-wan · Kurobe · Iiyama · Jōshin'etsu-kōgen National Park · Takaoka · Oyabe · Toyama · Obuse · Numata · Kanazawa · Chubū-Sangaku Nat Park · Ōmachi · Nagano · Komatsu · Kamioka · 2560m · Ueda · Maebashi · Kiryū · Kaga · Ogimachi · Shirakawa Hirayu 3190m · Matsumoto · Takasaki · Saku · Fujioka · Eiheiji Temple · Hakusan Nat Park · onsen · Kamikōchi · Fukui · Katsuyama · Takayama · Shiojiri · Okaya · Suwa · Chichibu-Tama National Park · Tōkyō · Takefu · Ōno · Kanto-sanchi · Kyoga-misaki · Kanayama · Ina · 3192m · Kofu · Tango-hantō · Wakasa-wan · Ama-no-hashidate · Tsuruga · Nakatsugawa · Minami · Fuji-Hakone-Izu Nat Park · Tōkyō · Toyo'oka · Miyazu · Obama · Gifu · Kakamigahara · Alps National Park · 3776m · Odawara · Fukuchiyama · Maizuru · Tamba-kochi · Ōgaki · Inuyama · Ena · Fuji-san · Ayabe · Biwa-ko · Komaki · Toki · Fujinomiya · Hikone · Ichinomiya · Kasugai · Fuji · Hakone · Kasai · Ōtsu · Kusatsu · Kuwana · NAGOYA · Tōkai · Toyota · Shizuoka · Numazu · Atami · KYŌTO · Yokkaichi · Kariya · Okazaki · Tenryu · Fujieda · Shimizu · Itō · Takarazuka · Takatsuki · Uji · Kameyama · Suzuka · Toyohama · Kakegawa · Yaizu · Fuji-Hakone-Izu Nat Park · Amagasaki · Hirakata · Tsu · Mikawa-wan · Hamana-ko · Izu-hantō · Akashi · KŌBE · Sakai · Ueno · Nabari · Matsusaka · Hamamatsu · Shimoda · Izumi · Horyuji Temple · Nara · Ise · Omae-zaki · Irō-zaki · Ōsaka-wan · Kishiwada · Kashihara · Toba · Ise-Shima National Park · Kozū-jima · Sumoto · Gojō · Ago · Daiō-zaki · Enshū-nada · Wakayama · Ōmine-san 1915m · Yoshino-Kumano · Kōya-san · Owase · National Park · Gobo · Kii-hantō · Kumano · Tanabe · Nachi Falls · Shingu · Kii Katsuura · Shio-no-misaki

0 · 50 · 100 km

Heian Shrine is a replica of the first imperial palace in Kyoto, Japan's ancient capital

The old capital, Kyoto, will be the highlight of any visit to Japan; but the whole area is rich in history and culture. South of Kyoto is Nara, an older capital still, and the rolling hills of Asuka, where the ancient Japanese first settled in the 7th century. To the north are the Japan Alps and the rugged Japan Sea coast. The area also includes three vibrant cities, Osaka, Kobe and Nagoya. Though Kobe was devastated in the January 1995 earthquake, rebuilding is already nearly completed.

In September 1994 Kansai International Airport opened off the coast of Osaka. The people of Central Japan are sure that this will bring in a new period of prosperity for the area.

Kyoto

*K*yoto's history began in 794 when Emperor Kammu (737–806) made his new capital here. When, after more than 1,000 years, the centre of power shifted to Tokyo under the shoguns, Kyoto remained the home of emperors and a repository of classical culture.

Kyoto is well worth a long and leisurely visit. This is a living city, with industry and traffic-clogged streets, but you will soon discover the treasures hidden behind the modern façade. Of 1,650 Buddhist temples, some are grand and imposing, others peaceful and serene. Many were initially built as palaces, and within the wooden walls are sumptuously decorated rooms. There are also 400 Shinto shrines, 60 gardens, three imperial palaces and several museums.

This is a city which repays exploring on foot. Kyoto escaped bombing during the war, and there are streets full of mellow old houses and shops selling traditional handicrafts. The streets are laid out on a grid plan, with all roads running north–south or east–west, which makes it easy to find your way around. Distances are often further than you think. Most sights are accessible only by bus, but a rudimentary subway system runs up the middle of the city.

Dialling code: 075
Tourist Information Centre (TIC), Karasuma Street, opposite Kyoto station (tel: 075 371 5649). Open: 9am–5pm Monday to Friday, 9am–noon Saturday.

1 hour from Kansai International Airport and 2½ hours from Tokyo by train.

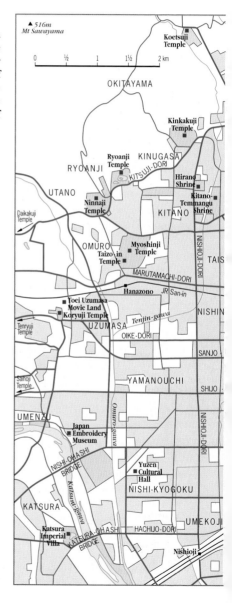

KYOTO CITY MAP

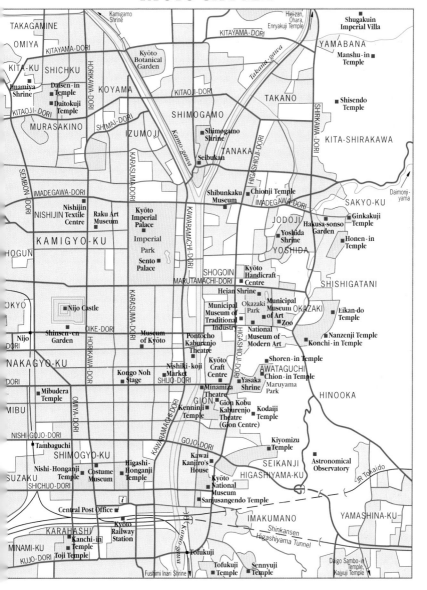

The elegant Ginkakuji (Silver Pavilion) with its stunning raked sand gardens

DAITOKUJI

Many people's favourite Zen temple, Daitokuji is a complex of 24 sub-temples, each with its own character, history and garden. Only a few are open to the public. Others you can enter to study Zen meditation, while some serve Buddhist vegetarian meals on Sundays. Daisen-in has the most famous garden – go early or late in the day to avoid the crowds and appreciate the exquisite perfection of the rocks, sand and moss that create a whole universe in a tiny space. Don't miss the beautiful ink paintings.

North Kyoto, few minutes' bus ride from Kitaoji subway. Grounds always open. Subtemples open: daily, 9am–4.30pm, last entry 4pm. Admission charge.

ENRYAKUJI

The atmospheric temple buildings of Enryakuji are in a splendid mountain setting, spread across the entire top of Mount Hiei. Enryakuji was founded in 806 to protect Kyoto from evil spirits, thought to come from the northeast. At its height there were 3,000 sub-temples, housing thousands of fierce warrior monks. In time the monks became a scourge rather than a blessing. Whenever they disagreed with the emperor, they would descend in force on the city, raiding rival monasteries, burning scriptures and killing the priests. Finally, in 1571, the warlord Nobunaga Oda stormed the mountain, burnt down the temples and killed the monks. More than 100 temples have been rebuilt. The majestic main hall, Kompon Chu-do, dates from 1642.

Northeast of Kyoto, bus from Kyoto station or Keihan Sanjo station. Tel: 0775 78 0551. Grounds always open; admission free. Kompon Chu-do open: daily, 8.30am–4.30pm March to November, 9am–4pm in winter. Admission charge.

FUSHIMI INARI TAISHA
(Fushimi Inari Shrine)

This shrine, dating from the 8th century, is the most important of the 40,000 shrines dedicated to Inari, god of rice, *sake* and prosperity. Businessmen come in their thousands to pray for success and wealth. After encountering an enormous red *torii*, then shrine buildings flanked by stone foxes (the fox is Inari's representative on earth), you begin to climb. The entire hillside is covered in countless red *torii*, pressed together to form endless tunnels; you walk in a strange red twilight, occasionally emerging at a small shrine on a rocky outcrop.

South Kyoto, at Inari station. Always open. Admission free.

GINKAKUJI (Silver Pavilion)

The exquisite Silver Pavilion is one of Kyoto's most famous sights – though in fact it was never silver. It was built as a pleasure villa for Shogun Yoshimasa in 1492, but Japan was so impoverished by civil war that there were no funds to carry out the plan to cover the building in silver. Instead it is of dark wood, with a phoenix perched on the roof. In front is a raked sand garden, and beyond that paths climb the wooded hillside, between waterfalls and ponds full of carp. Like his grandfather Shogun Yoshimitsu Ashikaga, builder of the Golden Pavilion (see page 81), Yoshimasa was a great patron of the arts. Within the temple grounds is the famous Dojin-sai, Japan's first ever tea ceremony room; apply in writing to view it.

East Kyoto, bus to Ginkakuji-michi. Tel: 075 771 5725. Open: daily, 8.30am–5pm 15 March to 30 November, 9am–4.30pm in winter. Admission charge.

GION

Gion is Kyoto's legendary geisha district. In the daytime, you can stroll down Hanami-koji and admire the 17th-century restaurants and teahouses. But the area really comes alive in the early evening. Lanterns gleam, lights glow softly behind the paper windows, and you may see *maiko* – trainee geisha – hurrying to work.

Central Kyoto, 5 minutes east of Keihan-Shijo station, off Shijo street.

A brightly lit shrine in Gion, the famous geisha quarter of Kyoto

The original Kinkakuji (Golden Pavilion) was burnt down by a mad monk

GOSHO (Kyoto Imperial Palace)

At the heart of the city, the Imperial Palace was the home of the emperor until the mid-19th century, and each new emperor returns for his investiture. The austere buildings, which date from 1855, contrast with the lavishness of the shogun's residence, Nijo Castle, just down the road (see page 84). There are several palaces within the compound, linked by corridors or galleries and separated by graceful gardens. The great hall is where the enthronement takes place.

Central Kyoto, 10 minutes' walk south of Imadegawa subway. Tours at 9am, 11am, 1.30pm, 3pm. Apply at Imperial Household Agency near the gate (tel: 211 1215), with your passport, at least 20 minutes before tour. Admission free.

HEIAN SHRINE

Heian Shrine evokes the first Kyoto – Heian-kyo, the Capital of Peace and Tranquillity, founded in 794. The shrine itself was built in 1895, and is dedicated to the first and last emperors to reign in Kyoto. Its brilliant vermilion buildings, with their green-tiled roofs, are a two-thirds scale replica of the original Heian-period Imperial Palace. In spring, people flock to see the cherry blossoms in the beautifully landscaped gardens.

Central Kyoto, 10 minutes north of Dobutsuen-mae bus stop. Open: daily, 8.30am–5.30pm 15 March to 31 August; 8.30am–5pm 1–14 March and September to October; 8.30am–4.30pm November to February. Admission charge to garden; admission to shrine free.

KATSURA RIKYU (Katsura Imperial Villa)

The exquisite perfection of the Katsura Imperial Villa with its elegant landscaped gardens gives some idea of the life of the aristocracy in the time of the shoguns. Completed over 50 years, beginning in

YUKIO MISHIMA

Yukio Mishima (1925–70) is famous as much for his spectacular death as for his brilliant writing. The author of an enormous variety of intense, tormented novels, poetry and plays, Mishima published his first works when he was still at university. One of his most famous novels is _Kinkakuji_ (_The Temple of the Golden Pavilion_), the story of the young monk who became obsessed with the beauty of the Golden Pavilion and burnt it down. Mishima ended his own life with a samurai-style _seppuku_ (ritual suicide), having tried and failed to bring about a right-wing revolution.

perfectly reflected in the water. The walls, pillars and eaves of the top two floors are entirely covered in gold leaf. On the pinnacle of the roof is a golden phoenix. Built in 1394, Kinkakuji was originally a pleasure pavilion for Shogun Yoshimitsu. On his death, it was made into a Zen temple. In 1950 a young monk burnt it to the ground; the present building is a faithful reconstruction.

Northwest Kyoto, near Ryoanji, accessible by bus. Tel: 461 0013. Open: daily, 9am–5.30pm; 9am–5pm October to March. Admission charge.

Heian shrine, modelled on the first imperial palace, takes us back a thousand years

1590, the villa was built for an aesthete brother of the emperor and is considered one of the pinnacles of Japanese architecture. There are teahouses, moon-viewing pavilions, a music room and a veranda for watching _kemari_, a football game played at court. The superb gardens were designed by the great Japanese landscape architect Kobori Enshu, who is said to have accepted the job on two conditions: unlimited time and unlimited funds.

Southwest Kyoto, accessible by bus or train to Katsura station. Tours at 10am and 2pm. Apply at least one day in advance (preferably well before) at Imperial Household Agency in Imperial Palace grounds (tel: 211 1215), with your passport. Admission free.

KINKAKUJI (Golden Pavilion)

The fabulous Golden Pavilion is top of many visitors' sightseeing list for Kyoto. Surprisingly small and delicate, it stands perched on the edge of a large lake,

Kiyomizu is famous for its sacred waters, which are said to have healing properties

KITANO-TEMMANGU SHRINE

This splendid old shrine is dedicated to Sugawara no Michizane, the 9th-century scholar who was deified as Tenjin, the god of learning (see page 133). The gardens are planted with plum trees, his favourite flower, and there is a large bronze ox, his animal guardian. The shrine is particularly famous for its flea market, held on the 25th of each month. On that day the Tenjin Engi Scrolls, depicting the legend of Michizane, are on view.

Central Kyoto, north of Nijo Castle, accessible by bus. Open: daily, sunrise to sunset. Admission free.

KIYOMIZU TEMPLE

No matter how many times you see Kiyomizu, you always come upon it with a sense of discovery. It is the most spectacular of structures, the vast thatched temple buildings standing on a scaffolding of immense wooden pillars, looking out across the city.

Kiyomizu – meaning 'Pure Water' – was founded in 798. During its long and turbulent history it was burnt down several times; the present buildings date from 1633. The weather-worn temple buildings are immensely atmospheric. From the main hall, steps lead down to Otawa waterfall, whose pure waters give the temple its name and are said to have therapeutic properties. Visitors stop to drink or even stand underneath. The small three-storeyed pagoda on the opposite hill gives a wonderful view of the whole temple.

East Kyoto, accessible by bus. Tel: 551 1234. Open: daily, 6am–6pm. Admission charge.

KYOTO KOKURITSU HAKUBUTSUKAN (Kyoto National Museum)

As one would expect in this city of temples, the Kyoto National Museum focuses on Buddhist art. The fine collection is shown in chronological order, beginning with ceramics and burial urns from the earliest historical periods, and includes a hall of gigantic

GEISHA

Along the lantern-lit streets of Gion or Pontocho, you might see a geisha or a *maiko* (a trainee geisha), flitting along like a butterfly in a colourful kimono, on high wooden clogs, face exquisitely painted. Do not imagine that a geisha is a prostitute. They are ladies of the evening, not ladies of the night, trained in the arts of music and dancing, adept at charming shy Japanese males with their girlish conversation. Today, in Kyoto, young women still learn the art of the geisha, and geisha still entertain wealthy clients behind closed doors.

bronze Buddhist images, black and white ink brush paintings, gold screens and calligraphy. Besides priceless Japanese works, there are Chinese ceramics and paintings which were collected by temples and were often a major inspiration for local artists.
Southeast Kyoto, opposite Sanjusangendo. Tel: 541 1151. Open 9am–4.30pm, last entry 4pm; closed Monday. Admission charge.

NANZENJI

This famous and imposing Zen temple spreads across the foothills of Higashiyama, the 'Eastern Mountains'. Visitors come to study Zen, to dine on *yudofu* (simmered tofu, a Kyoto speciality served in small shops around the temple grounds) or simply to admire the buildings. Nanzenji's symbol is its massive two-storey gate, the Sanmon; from the upper floor there are fine views across the city. Its glory is the palatial abbot's quarters, once part of the Kyoto imperial palace, given to the temple in

Kyoto's National Museum, which concentrates on Buddhist art, dates from the Meiji period

1611. The many rooms are decorated with lavish paintings – ink paintings of bamboos and pine, paintings on gold leaf of tigers frolicking. At the centre is the Leaping Tiger garden, a serene space of raked sand and rocks, one of which resembles a leaping tiger.
East Kyoto, accessible by bus or tram to Keage station. Tel: 771 0365. Open: daily, 8am–5pm April to October, 8am–5.30pm November to March. Admission charge.

The country's most skilled artisans laboured to decorate every inch of Nijo Castle

NIJO-JO (Nijo Castle)

Nijo Castle, with its sumptuous rooms full of paintings glimmering with gold leaf, was the Kyoto residence of the shoguns. You enter through the huge and ornately carved front gates, then pass through a series of audience chambers. Common people could go no further than the first, decorated with lavish paintings, friezes and coffered ceilings to impress upon them the shogun's power. The inner halls were for those of higher rank; here the decoration is subtler but even more costly. Ever wary of treachery, the shoguns installed 'nightingale floors', which creak under the lightest tread to warn of intruders. There were no trees in the magnificent landscaped gardens: the shoguns did not want to see the falling leaves and be reminded of their own mortality.

Central Kyoto, bus or Oike subway. Tel: 841 0096. Open: daily, 8.45am–5pm, last entry 4pm. Admission charge.

NINNAJI

This grand old temple had a retired emperor as its first abbot and he was succeeded by imperial princes until the Meiji era. Founded in 886, the temple burnt down and was rebuilt in the 1630s. The splendid main hall was originally part of the imperial palace and houses an image of the Buddha Amida from 888. The spacious grounds are full of cherry trees; people come in April to admire the blossom.

Northwest Kyoto, near Ryoanji, accessible by bus. Open: daily, 9am–5pm; 9am–4.30pm in winter. Admission charge.

NISHI HONGANJI

Some of Kyoto's most spectacular sights are hidden here. Visitors are free to explore the vast outer halls, built to accommodate thousands of worshippers, but to see the real treasures you must apply in advance. The inner chambers are breathtaking. Brought from Fushimi Castle, palace of the 16th-century warlord Hideyoshi Toyotomi, they are decorated in the lavish Momoyama style. Sliding doors open to reveal chamber after chamber, glowing with gold. Every surface of the screens, transoms and coffered ceilings is covered in gold leaf, painted with landscapes, pine trees and birds. The oldest *noh* stage in existence, dating from 1581, is also here.
South Kyoto, 10 minutes' walk northwest of Kyoto station. Tel: 371 5180. Tours of inner chambers: Monday to Friday 10am, 11am, 1.30pm, 2.30pm; Saturday 10am, 11am (apply in advance). Admission free.

OHARA

From Kyoto a single road winds north through the hills to the tiny village of Ohara. Jakko-in, west of the village, is a secluded nunnery at the top of a long flight of rough stone steps, enclosed by steep hills. In 1185 the Empress Kenreimon-in was incarcerated here, after a long war in which she had seen her whole family killed and her baby son – the heir to the empire – drowned. The atmospheric old temple and mossy gardens are said to be exactly as they were in her day. Sanzen-in Temple, to the east, has beautiful grounds brilliant with maple leaves in autumn. The main hall houses three great 10th-century images: the Buddha Amida accompanied by two Bodhisattvas.
Northeast of Kyoto, accessible by bus.

Jakko-in open: daily, 9am–5pm March to November, 9am–4.30pm in winter, last entry 30 minutes before close. Admission charge. Sanzen-in open: daily, 8.30am–5.30pm March to November, 8.30am–5pm in winter. Admission charge.

PONTOCHO

At night, Pontocho is one of Kyoto's liveliest areas. This small pedestrian alley running alongside the river has some prohibitively expensive geisha establishments – it is Kyoto's number two geisha district, after Gion (see page 79) – but also plenty of cheaper, casual restaurants. In summer you can dine on a veranda over the river.
Central Kyoto, west of the river, between Keihan-Shijo and Keihan-Sanjo stations.

Even during the daylight hours, Pontocho's neon lights are dazzling!

ZEN BUDDHISM AND GARDENS

'What is the sound of one hand clapping?' Conundrums like this – called *koan* – are one of the ways by which Zen monks try to bypass the conscious thinking mind in their quest for enlightenment.

Zen Buddhism reached Japan from India by way of China in 1192, when the priest Eisai founded the first Zen temples here. It appealed to the samurai, with their soldier's code of austerity, and quickly permeated Japanese life. It inspired the tea ceremony, the aesthetic of simplicity, the emphasis on iron self-control – you could say that Zen is the soul of Japan.

In essence, Zen is the belief that truth is to be found inside, not outside, the seeker. Zen monks lead a life of austerity, owning nothing, eating seldom. They meditate for several hours a day, gazing at a wall, looking deep inside themselves, striving for *satori*, the experience of enlightenment.

Zen gardens are a celebrated expression of the Zen way. Stark and tranquil, they consist simply of dark rocks set,

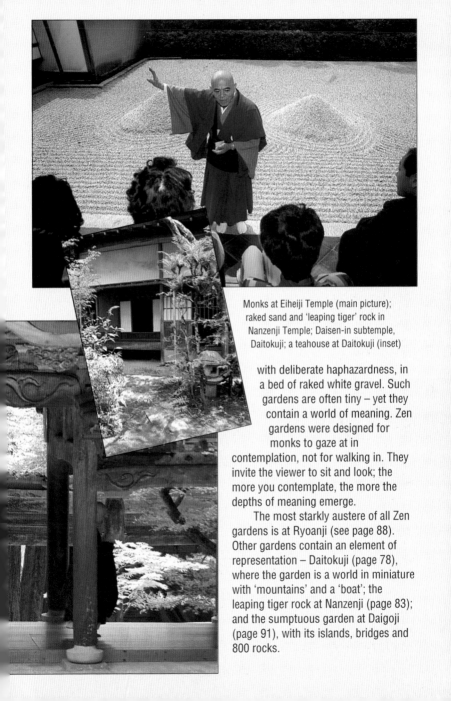

Monks at Eiheiji Temple (main picture); raked sand and 'leaping tiger' rock in Nanzenji Temple; Daisen-in subtemple, Daitokuji; a teahouse at Daitokuji (inset)

with deliberate haphazardness, in a bed of raked white gravel. Such gardens are often tiny – yet they contain a world of meaning. Zen gardens were designed for monks to gaze at in contemplation, not for walking in. They invite the viewer to sit and look; the more you contemplate, the more the depths of meaning emerge.

The most starkly austere of all Zen gardens is at Ryoanji (see page 88). Other gardens contain an element of representation – Daitokuji (page 78), where the garden is a world in miniature with 'mountains' and a 'boat'; the leaping tiger rock at Nanzenji (page 83); and the sumptuous garden at Daigoji (page 91), with its islands, bridges and 800 rocks.

RYOANJI

The garden at Ryoanji is the ultimate Zen garden – an expanse of white sand, perfectly raked, surrounding 15 rocks. The best way to appreciate it is to sit quietly and let the meaning unfold. Don't miss the quiet graveyard behind the temple, with a lake and a view across Kyoto. Go early to avoid the crowds.

Northwest Kyoto, near Kinkakuji and Ninnaji, accessible by bus. Tel: 463 2216. Open: daily, 8am–5pm January to November, 8.30am–4.30pm December. Admission charge.

SAIHOJI

Entering Saihoji's moss garden is like stepping into an enchanted forest. Designed in 1339 by the great Zen priest Soseki Muso (1275–1351), it was once as austere as Ryoanji's garden. Then moss began to grow. There are now more than 100 varieties, forming a richly textured carpet beneath the glowing maples and giving the place its popular name, Kokedera (Moss Temple).

Its many visitors began to threaten the delicate garden, and now application to see it must be made at least one week in advance (Kyoto TIC has details). You pay a hefty admission charge and chant sutras (Buddhist scriptures) or do Zen meditation for one hour. But the garden makes it all worthwhile.

Southwest Kyoto, near Katsura, accessible by bus. Tel: 391 3631. Tours at 10am and 1pm. Admission charge.

SANJUSANGENDO

This awe-inspiring temple, founded in 1164 and rebuilt in 1266 after it burnt down, is really a vast altar, with 1,001 images of Kannon, the deity of mercy, standing rank upon rank in the gloom. The central image, a huge 1,000-armed Kannon, is particularly fine. The enormously long veranda is used for an annual archery contest.

Southeast Kyoto, opposite Museum. Tel:

Some of the thousand and one images of the deity Kannon in Sanjusangendo Temple

The impressive thousand-armed Kannon image of Sanjusangendo

561 3334. *Open: 8am–4.30pm 1 April to 15 November, 9am–3.30pm in winter. Admission charge.*

SHUGAKUIN RIKYU (Shugakuin Imperial Villa)

Set in the hills overlooking the city, the villa and its gardens – surely the most spectacular in Japan – were designed in the 1650s for the retired Emperor Go-Mizuno-o. Dotted about the grounds are pavilions and teahouses where he passed his days moon-gazing and composing poetry. From the streams and tinkling cascades of the Lower Garden, you climb along a tree-lined path to the Middle Garden. The pavilion here has a famous painting of fish, so lifelike that the artist painted a net over them to prevent them from swimming away. Finally you reach the Rin'un-tei ('pavilion in the clouds') and a breathtaking panorama: the Upper Garden, with its lake, bridges, waterfalls, islands and exquisite pavilions, forms the foreground; behind is the city of Kyoto, with range upon range of mountains. *Northeast Kyoto, en route to Ohara and Enryakuji, accessible by bus. Tours at 9am, 10am, 11am, 1.30pm, 3pm Monday to Friday; 9am, 10am, 11am Saturday. Apply well in advance at Imperial Household Agency in Imperial Palace grounds (tel: 211 1215), with passport. Admission free.*

TOJI

Toji's five-storey pagoda, at 57m the tallest in the country, is a symbol of Kyoto. This splendid old temple houses some marvellous art, including a celebrated 9th-century three-dimensional mandala (Buddhist symbol of the universe) made up of 21 images. Toji is famous for its flea market, held on the 21st of each month. *Southern Kyoto, 15 minutes' walk southwest of station. Open: daily, 9am–4.30pm. Admission charge.*

Kyoto Environs

Some of Kyoto's most famous and ancient buildings are not in the city itself but some distance away to the south.

UJI

The small town of Uji is famous above all for its tea, considered the best in Japan. But 1,000 years ago, this pretty area – surrounded by gently-rolling hills and on a rushing river, some 20km from Kyoto on the road to Nara – was where princes and nobles built their country villas. Later many were turned into temples, of which one, the Byodo-in, survives.

Byodo-in (Phoenix Hall)

Look on your Y10 coin and you will see the Byodo-in. This exquisite structure was built in 1053 and has survived in its pristine beauty for nearly 1,000 years. Designed as an earthly imitation of the Western Paradise, it was built to resemble a phoenix. The two verandas,

on delicate pillars, stretch to each side like wings, the corridor at the back forms the tail. On the roof are two bronze phoenixes. The whole building stands, extraordinarily light and ethereal, poised above the surrounding lake.

The hall houses a statue of Amida, Buddha of compassion and ruler of the Western Paradise. Commoners were not allowed to enter, so the builders inserted a window in the latticework. From across the lake you can see Amida's face, perfectly framed, gazing benevolently out. The vast statue is made of wood, lacquered and gilded, surrounded by an intricately carved golden halo. Adorning the walls are 52 heavenly beings seated

The exquisite Byodo-in (Phoenix Hall), one of Japan's oldest buildings

on clouds, playing musical instruments. On the doors and wooden walls are delicate paintings, some of the oldest in Japan.

Within the temple complex, the Kannon-do dates from the 13th century and houses an image of Kannon, the deity of mercy. There is also a treasure-house where you can see the weather-worn original phoenix finials.

10 minutes' walk from Uji station. Tel: 0774 21 2861. Open: daily, 8.30am–5.30pm March to November, 9am–4pm in winter. Admission charge.

Daigoji

Daigoji's picturesque grounds spread across a mountainside and include Kyoto's oldest building, a five-storey pagoda (951). You can stroll along an avenue lined with cherry trees, past temples and ponds, then climb the pilgrims' path to the temple buildings at the top of the hill.

The glory of the temple is a much later development, the sub-temple of Sambo-in. Remodelled in 1598 on the instructions of Toyotomi Hideyoshi (see page 10), Sambo-in is a supreme example of the great general's taste for opulence and luxury. Room after room is walled with exquisite painted screens. The whole complex of buildings focuses on the lavish garden, with its wide pond, moss-covered stone bridges and nearly 800 rocks.

Southeast of Kyoto, en route to Uji (20 minutes); 10 minutes' bus ride from Rokujizo station (alight at Samboin-mae). Tel: 075 571 0002. Grounds always open.

Ornate arrangements of nature in Sambo-in gardens, at a sub-temple of Daigoji

Sambo-in open: daily, 9am–5pm March to October, 9am–4pm in winter. Admission charge.

Mampukuji

Mampukuji is a Chinese Zen temple – one of the very few in Japan – founded by the Chinese Zen master Ingen in the 17th century and built in Ming dynasty style. The temple buildings incorporate elements of Chinese design and contain images of vigorous plump-faced Bodhisattvas like elderly cherubs, utterly unlike Japanese images. Mampukuji is a living, working monastery with a community of monks. It is also famous for its cuisine: if you book beforehand you can try Chinese Buddhist vegetarian dishes in the temple's dining hall.

South of Kyoto, en route to Uji; 5 minutes' walk from Obaku station. Tel: 0774 32 3900. Open: daily, 9am–4.30pm. Admission charge.

Uji is 40–50 minutes south of Kyoto by train.

Higashiyama

This stroll through the picturesque back streets of Higashiyama (the 'Eastern Mountains') in south-east Kyoto begins near the city's best-loved temple and ends at the huge and colourful Heian Shrine. *Allow 3 hours.*

Take the bus to Umamachi, then walk round the block to Kawai Kanjiro's house; or take a taxi.

1 KAWAI KANJIRO KINENKAN (Kawai Kanjiro's House)

Kawai Kanjiro (1890–1966) was a potter who produced wonderful, idiosyncratic works. Some of his pots are exhibited in his large and beautiful house, along with his folk art collection and wood-fired kiln.
From the main road, Gojo-dori, cross under the expressway to Gojozaka, the narrow paved road beyond a large temple gate.

2 KIYOMIZU TEMPLE

Gojozaka – the quiet way to approach this most popular of temples – leads steeply uphill past a stonemason's workshop specialising in gravestones. Many of your fellow walkers have come to place flowers on the graves of their dead: as you climb higher you see that the hillside is covered in tombs. Walk up some steps and suddenly, magically, Kiyomizu Temple (see page 82) is before you.
From Kiyomizu, take Kiyomizu-michi, the lively street at the front gate of the temple.

3 SANNENZAKA AND NINENZAKA

Among the many souvenir shops are pottery shops specialising in *Kiyomizu* porcelain and stoneware. Watch for cobbled steps leading down to your right to Sannenzaka, a charming street lined with willow trees, old wooden shops, houses and small teahouses. Soon another set of steps, marked by a signpost

A 19th-century replica of the first imperial palace in Japan: Heian Shrine

in English for 'Maruyama Park', leads to your right, down to Ninenzaka, with craft shops and restaurants. At the end of Ninenzaka is a main road. On the hillside to your right is an enormous concrete statue of Kannon, deity of mercy, a memorial to the World War II dead.
Cross the main road and walk north, skirting Kodaiji, with gardens and teahouses. Carry straight on to Maruyama Park. A red torii on your left marks the entrance to Yasaka Shrine.

4 YASAKA JINJA (Yasaka Shrine)
Yasaka's red-painted buildings are particularly evocative in the evening, lit with thousands of paper lanterns. The history of this splendid old shrine is obscure but it is always full of worshippers. It serves the nearby Gion area (see page 79) and organises the annual Gion festival (see pages 158–9).
Return to Maruyama Park and walk on northwards.

5 HEIAN SHRINE
Your walk takes you past the huge, ornately carved Sanmon Gate of Chion-in Temple, the largest temple gate in Japan. Drop in to see the equally massive temple buildings, with some fine, painted screens and a huge and famous temple bell. Beyond Chion-in is Shoren-in Temple, with two beautiful gardens. Cross Sanjo-dori, with its tram lines leading into the centre of town. Ahead of you is a gigantic *torii*. Cross the red-painted bridge to Heian Shrine (see page 80).
From Heian Shrine take the Chin-chin bus back to the city centre or the station. Or cut back towards the hills, to Nanzenji; from there follow the Philosopher's Path along the foot of the mountains to Ginkakuji.

Kawai Kanjiro Kinenkan – Tel: 561 3585. Open: 10am–5pm; closed Monday, 10–20 August. Admission charge.
Chion-in Temple – Open: 9am–4.30pm March to November, 9am–4pm December to February. Admission charge.
Shoren-in Temple – Open: daily, 9am–5pm. Admission charge.

Arashiyama

This is a gentle stroll through bamboo groves at the foot of the Arashiyama hills in western Kyoto, taking in old temples, a rustic hermitage and a splendid imperial palace-turned-temple. Arashiyama is particularly popular in autumn, when the maple trees are a blaze of colour. *Allow half a day.*

Take a bus or train to Arashiyama. From Togetsu-kyo ('Moon-crossing Bridge'), you can take a punt down the river and, in July and August, watch cormorant fishing. Walk away from the river; Tenryuji is on your left, through a huge wooden gateway, at the end of a tree-lined path.

1 TENRYUJI

The temple was founded in 1339 after a priest dreamed of a dragon rising from the nearby river – *ten-ryu* means 'heavenly dragon'. The original buildings have disappeared but the celebrated 14th-century garden designed by Muso (see **Saihoji**, page 88) remains. At the centre is a lake shaped like the character for 'heart', surrounded by raked sand, rocks and pines, with the hills of Arashiyama as the backdrop.

From the back (north) exit, follow the path through a bamboo grove. The road goes uphill and round to the right, past a small pond to another old wooden gate.

Tenryuji – Tel: 881 1235. Open: daily, 8.30am–5.30pm April to September, 8.30am–5pm in winter. Admission charge.
Jojakoji – Tel: 861 0435. Open: daily, 9am–5pm. Admission charge.
Rakushisha – Open: daily, 9am–5pm. Admission charge.
Adashino Nembutsuji – Tel: 861 2221. Open: daily, 9am–4.30pm March to November, 9.30am–4pm in winter. Admission charge.
Daikakuji – Tel: 871 0071. Open: daily, 9am–5pm. Admission charge.

Crowds stroll along the Hozu river in Arashiyama, 'Storm Mountain'

2 JOJAKOJI

The atmospheric old temple belongs to the Nichiren sect of Buddhism. You can wander the cobbled paths along mossy tree-clad slopes, dotted with weathered wooden buildings.

Take the first paved road on your left; turn right just beyond a vegetable field. Rakushisha is on your left.

3 RAKUSHISHA

This idyllic little hut, with its steep thatched roof, paper doors and decorative bamboo fence, was where the poet Basho stayed when he visited Kyoto. Looking out on to the hills of Arashiyama, he wrote one of his last works, *Saga Diary*.

Return to the road and follow it past several temples (about 10 minutes). Carry on up as the road becomes narrower and steeper. Cobbled steps lead off to your left to Nembutsuji.

4 ADASHINO NEMBUTSUJI

This hushed, rather haunting temple is packed with gravestones. Centuries ago, Adashino was a burial ground for all the nameless common folk not grand enough to be honoured with a tomb. The many stone Buddhas scattered around the countryside were assembled here so that prayers could be offered for their souls.

Retrace your steps and take the main road on your left. Follow the road round past Seiryoji to Daikakuji.

5 DAIKAKUJI

Daikakuji was built as a palace for the 9th-century Emperor Saga. Pressed against the mountainside, it overlooks a limpid lake, Osawa Pond. Later it was turned into a temple. The present, still palatial buildings date from the 16th century. You can stroll along the broad verandas beneath the spreading eaves, admire the sliding doors covered in gold leaf and painted with peonies and plum trees, and feed the carp in Osawa Pond.

From Daikakuji there are buses back to Kyoto Station and central Kyoto.

EIHEIJI, FUKUI

This ancient and famous Zen temple was founded in 1244 by Dogen, who brought the Zen teachings from China to Japan. It is a living, working temple, where Zen monks meditate, sleep, garden and eat simple vegetarian meals. For visitors Eiheiji provides a glimpse of this austere lifestyle.

The temple complex is arranged with impressive symmetry across the lower slopes of a mountain. The three most important rooms, where monks are forbidden to speak, are the toilet, the bath and the living and meditating quarters. There is also a splendid Buddha Hall, which enshrines images of the three Buddhas of past, present and future; an imposing main gate, with carved guardian deities; and the mausoleum, containing the ashes of Dogen.

Many westerners come here for a taste of Zen training for a few days, a few weeks – or a few years. To do so, apply (by telephone or in writing) at least two weeks in advance.
Fukui: 50 minutes southwest of Kanazawa, 1½ hours northeast of Kyoto by train. Eiheiji is 35 minutes east of Fukui by train. Eiheiji-cho, Yoshida-gun, Fukui-ken 910-12. Tel: 0776 63 3102. Open: daily, dawn to 3.30pm. Admission charge.

GIFU

Gifu, surrounded by wooded hills, is a small, pleasant city spreading across the valley of the river Nagara. It is famous for cormorant fishing. Every fine night between 11 May and 15 October, fishermen in traditional grass skirts and peaked black hats drift downriver in small boats with a flotilla of tame cormorants swimming alongside. Small, sweet trout – a delicacy – are attracted by the light of torches, and the cormorants dive in, catch the fish and bring them to the fishermen. For the onlookers in the surrounding boats it is primarily an opportunity for merrymaking.

Gifu also has the largest lacquer Buddha in Japan and two fine country temples, tucked away at the end of tram lines: Tanigumi, deep in the mountains, and Yokokura, famous for its mummified priests.
30 minutes north of Nagoya by train. Cormorant fishing: tickets available from hotels or directly (tel: 0582 62 0104). Tanigumi and Yokokura temples: 30–45 minutes by tram from Chusetsu Bridge terminal, Gifu. Open: daily, 9am–5pm. Admission free to grounds. Admission charge to see mummies.

HIKONE

As you walk from the station through Hikone's quiet streets, you can see the beautiful old castle on the hill in front of you, dominating the town. Completed in

---

BASHO AND *HAIKU*

Matsuo Basho (1644–94) was the quintessential Japanese poet. Born in Iga Ueno, he soon left his native town and took up the life of a wanderer. Like a Zen monk, he owned nothing and never married. His greatest achievement was to take the 17-syllable *haiku*, one of the classic forms of Japanese poetry, and make it into a fine art. Basho's finest *haiku* encapsulate a moment and all its philosophical ramifications in just a few words, as in the famous

'Old pond,
frog jumps in –
sound of water.'

The spacious halls of the ancient Eiheiji Zen Temple, where monks still live and work today

1622, it took nearly 20 years to build and is one of the finest castles in Japan. Much of the original, with its graceful structure and sweeping roofs, is still intact. From the upper floors you can look out across the placid waters of Lake Biwa. In spring, the park surrounding the castle is pink with cherry blossom. There is also an elegant landscaped garden, Genkyuen.

50 minutes northeast of Kyoto by train. Castle: 10 minutes' walk west of station. Tel: 0749 22 2954. Open: daily, 8.30am–5pm. Admission charge.

IGA UENO

In feudal times, the out-of-the-way town of Iga Ueno was the headquarters of the *ninja* (see box). Here they posed as farmers, living in farmhouses riddled with false floors, walls that were really revolving doors, hidden rooms and hoards of concealed weapons. One of these houses remains, its secrets revealed by young women clad in *ninja* outfits. Iga Ueno is also the birthplace of Japan's best-loved poet, Matsuo Basho.
1 hour east of Nara or 1½ hours southwest of Nagoya by train. Ninja House, in Ueno Park. Open: daily, 9am–5pm. Admission charge.

INUYAMA

Inuyama Castle (1440) is Japan's oldest. A charming, small castle with thick wooden beams and low-slung rafters, it was made entirely without nails. From the top floor there are fine views of the pretty town of Inuyama and Kiso river. Near by is Uraku-en Garden, with its exquisite teahouse.

Not far away is Meiji-mura, a village of Meiji period buildings,

moved here to preserve them. There is an old *kabuki* theatre, a bathhouse, merchants' houses, a steam train and tram, and Frank Lloyd Wright's original Imperial Hotel, which survived the 1923 Tokyo earthquake.
25 minutes north of Nagoya by train. Castle, 10 minutes' walk west of station. Open: daily, 9am–4.30pm. Uraku-en Garden, 5 minutes' walk from castle. Open: daily, 9am–5pm March to November, 9am–4pm in winter. Meiji-mura, 15 minutes from Inuyama by train and bus or 1 hour from Nagoya by direct bus. Tel: 0568 67 0314. Open: daily, 10am–5pm March to October, 10am–4pm in winter. Admission charge to all.

Fearsome *ninja* in Ninja House, Iga Ueno

NINJA

Spies and hired killers, the *ninja* were masters of the art of invisibility. They could travel at astonishing speed, could climb supposedly impregnable castle walls, and used a fearsome battery of weapons. No matter how well protected you thought you were, a *ninja*, dressed head to toe in black, might suddenly swing in through a window or hurl a barbed chain dipped in poison to wrap around your neck. *Ninjutsu* (the art of stealth) flourished in the 14th and 15th centuries, and is still being taught today, though you are unlikely to meet a real-life *ninja*.

ISE

The Grand Shrines at Ise are the most important of Japan's Shinto shrines. They house the sacred mirror, one of the three imperial regalia, and the emperor worships here after his enthronement. In the past every Japanese tried to make the pilgrimage to Ise at least once in a lifetime.

Following Shinto tradition, the shrines are rebuilt afresh every 20 years, exactly as they were when first erected countless centuries earlier (the last rebuilding was in 1993). Ise is the only shrine which preserves this tradition.

Geku (Outer Shrine), traditionally established in 478, is dedicated to the goddess of agriculture and industry. Gravel paths lead through an ancient forest to the shrine buildings. As is usual in Shinto, you cannot enter the abode of the gods, but you can see the buildings beyond the fence.

Naiku (Inner Shrine) is a bus ride from Geku, at the top of a street of shops lining the ancient pilgrimage route. After crossing a bridge of unpainted cypress, you come to a place where pilgrims wash in the sacred Isuzu river. The shrine buildings, of plain unvarnished wood, are perfect reproductions of 6th-century Japanese architecture, and said to be modelled on ancient storehouses. Amaterasu, the sun goddess and mythical ancestor of the

A Japanese woman decked out in festive costume at the Grand Shrines of Ise

imperial family is believed to be enshrined here (see also **Takachiho**, page 142).

1½ hours south of Nagoya by train. Geku: 10 minutes' walk west of station. Naiku: 15 minutes by bus from Geku. Open: daily, sunrise to sunset. Admission free.

SHINTO

You cannot be long in Japan without coming across a *torii*, the gateway that marks the entrance to a Shinto shrine and to the realm of the gods. Shrines are everywhere ('shrine' in this context means a Shinto place of worship, not a small household shrine). You find them on the tops of mountains, in ancient cedar forests and beside lakes – and also in Buddhist temples, in the middle of towns or on top of office blocks.

Shinto is Japan's most ancient religion. It is not so much a set of beliefs as a way of life. In Shinto all nature is sacred: the natural awe we feel in a splendid setting is expressed through the Shinto shrine erected there.

The Shinto deities – of which there are many – play a part in people's everyday lives. Each rules a different aspect of life, has a different animal messenger and inspires a different style of shrine architecture. Thus Inari, god of rice, prosperity and commercial success (many businessmen pray to him) has the fox as messenger and bright vermilion shrines.

Shinto: a floating shrine (main picture); Shinto priests in their full regalia prepare to beat the drums; a huge *torii* gate, familiar feature of the Japanese landscape; and a knotted rope marking out sacred ground

Anyone can pray to the Shinto gods – for health, business success, a marriage partner or safety on the road. When you approach a shrine, first wash your hands and mouth to purify yourself and toss a coin into the offering box – a Y5 coin is particularly auspicious. Then ring the bell which hangs above the shrine to wake the god, bow twice and clap your hands twice. This is the time to pray or make your wish. Afterwards bow twice again; when you step away, be careful not to turn your back on the shrine.

The oldest Shinto shrine is Izumo (see page 123). The Ise shrine (see page 99), dedicated to the emperor, is considered the most important. The most famous is Fushimi Inari Shrine in Kyoto (see page 78).

The famous stone lantern links earth and water in Kenroku-en Garden

the Maeda treasures – golden saddles and stirrups, the finest *Kutani* porcelain, and a life-sized pheasant incense burner. *Opposite Kenroku-en and Seisonkaku. Tel: 0762 31 7580. Open: daily, 9.30am–4.30pm. Admission charge.*

Kenroku-en Garden

This glorious garden, traditionally rated one of Japan's three most beautiful, was completed over a period of 200 years. The Maeda family's private garden, it is exquisitely composed to form a series of pictures – Misty Lake with its tortoise-shaped island, Morning Glory Teahouse, a waterfall plunging through woodland ... *15 minutes by bus from station. Tel: 0762 21 5850. Open: daily, 7am–6pm 1 March to 15 October; 8am–4.30pm in winter. Admission charge.*

KANAZAWA

This lively, attractive city is the cultural and business centre of the Japan Sea coast. In the time of the shoguns, it was the capital of the hugely wealthy Maeda clan, whose patronage made it a centre for *noh* theatre and for sumptuous crafts: *yuzen* dyeing for formal kimonos, *Kutani* porcelain, gold-leaf and lacquerware.

Kanazawa escaped bombing in the war, and much of the elegant old city, with its tiled roofs, remains. You can stroll the winding streets of Nagamachi, the old samurai area, and explore the pleasure quarters where you may still glimpse a geisha. The city's most famous sights are the legacy of the Maeda lords.

Ishikawa-mon (Ishikawa Gate)

Ishikawa Gate, virtually all that remains of Kanazawa Castle, gives some idea of how splendid the castle must have been. *At the entrance to Kanazawa University, opposite Kenroku-en.*

Ishikawa Kenritsu Bijutsukan (Ishikawa Prefectural Art Museum)

This excellent museum contains many of

Former teahouses in the geisha quarter of Kanazawa now serve as bars and restaurants

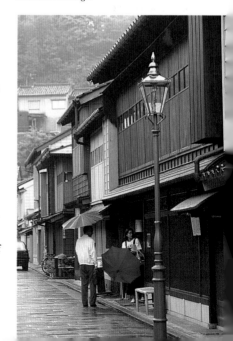

The port of Kobe, a cosmopolitan community which became the home of many westerners

Seisonkaku Villa

In 1863 the 13th Maeda lord built Seisonkaku as a retirement villa for his mother. The villa is the last word in opulence, full of exquisite ornamentation, with gold leaf dusting the sliding doors and coffered ceilings.
Beside Kenroku-en. Tel: 0762 21 0580. Open: 8.30am–4pm; closed Wednesday. Admission charge.

Kanazawa is 2¼ hours northeast of Kyoto and 4½ hours from Tokyo by train; or fly to Komatsu Airport. Information: Kanazawa International Exchange Foundation, 2-2-43 Nagamachi (tel: 0762 20 2522); also tourist information office in station.

KII-HANTO (Kii Peninsula)

The mountain fastnesses of the remote Kii Peninsula were for centuries the headquarters of ascetic mountaineering priests. At the heart is the sacred Mount Omine (see page 147). The whole area is quite spectacular – towering crags, plummeting gorges, Japan's highest waterfall (Nachi Falls), a wonderful hot spring inside a cave at Kii-Katsuura ... The coastal towns of Shingu and Kii Katsuura are linked to Osaka and Nagoya by rail; from there you travel by bus or rented car.
3 hours by express south of Nagoya or 4 hours from Osaka.

KOBE

Although devastated in the January 1995 earthquake, the port city of Kobe is now largely back to normal. It is famous for its cosmopolitan flavour. Many of the first westerners who came to Japan in the 19th century made their homes on the pleasant slopes of Mount Rokko and, with Chinese and Indian merchants, formed a busy international community. You can visit some of their houses in the Kitano-cho area, or take a cable car to the top of Rokko for views across the city and the Inland Sea.
15 minutes by ferry from Kansai International Airport; 15 minutes from Osaka and 30 minutes from Kyoto by train.

KOYA-SAN (Mount Koya)

A quintessential Japanese experience is a night in a Buddhist temple on Mount Koya, centre of the Shingon sect established by the priest and teacher Kobo Daishi. He founded the first monasteries on this mountaintop plateau in 816. In the Sacred Precinct is the Great Pagoda, the symbol of Koya-san; nearby Kongobuji has sumptuous 16th–century painted screens. Most impressive of all is the 1.5km-long cemetery, shaded by ancient cedars, where nearly every important person in Japanese history is buried. If you stay in a temple, you will be served lavish vegetarian cuisine and be awakened by the 5am call to prayers.

1½ hours south of Osaka by train. Koya-san Tourist Association, tel: 0736 56 2417.

MATSUMOTO

The black walls and tiled turrets of Matsumoto Castle rising above a lily-covered moat, with the snow-covered peaks of the Japan Alps as the backdrop, are a truly breathtaking sight. Completed in 1597, this is one of Japan's finest castles, second only to Himeji Castle (see page 122) in beauty and elegance of form. It was built to withstand real warfare and there are chutes for bombarding attackers and slots for arrows. The castle also has an exquisite 'moon-viewing turret'.

2 hours north of Nagoya by train; also accessible by plane. Matsumoto Castle, 20 minutes' walk northeast of station. Open: daily, 8.30am–5pm. Admission charge.

NAGANO

Nagano is the gateway to the Japan Alps and some of the most splendid countryside in Japan; people come to ski, hike and take the waters in the area's famous hot spring resorts. Nagano itself is a sleepy town – though rapidly changing in preparation for the Winter Olympics, due to take place here in 1998. Meanwhile millions of pilgrims come to worship at Zenkoji, a Buddhist temple founded in the 7th century. The wooden buildings are full of incense smoke and the murmuring of prayer. Follow the line of pilgrims shuffling into the dark recesses and you will be able to put your hand on the large, heavy key known as the 'key of paradise', believed to ensure salvation if touched.

2½ hours northwest of Tokyo by train. Zenkoji, 1.5km from station. Open: 24 hours. Admission free to temple; admission charge for inner sanctum and 'key of paradise'.

NAGOYA

Nagoya is Japan's fourth largest city, a major industrial metropolis; much of the nation's car industry is in the area. A centre for the aircraft and munitions industries during World War II, it was bombed flat. Today it is a large, vibrant city with modern buildings and wide streets – not beautiful, but with plenty of energy and life.

Nagoya was the birthplace of Japan's three great 16th-century warlords, the

Matsumoto's fine castle dominates the colourful streets below

last of whom, Ieyasu Tokugawa (see page 68), succeeded in unifying Japan. He built a formidable castle here in 1612 of which the present castle is a faithful reconstruction. While you are in the area, visit Atsuta shrine, one of the three most important shrines in Japan, repository for the Sacred Grass-mowing Sword, part of the imperial regalia. The Tokugawa Art Museum, containing the collection of the Tokugawa family, is also worth a visit. *2 hours west of Tokyo by train. Information Nagoya International Centre, tel: 052 581* *0100. Nagoya Castle, 5 minutes' walk from Shiyakusho subway. Tel: 052 231 1700. Open: daily, 9am–4.30pm. Admission charge. Atsuta Shrine, 5 minutes by train from Nagoya station. Always open. Admission free. Tokugawa Art Museum, 20 minutes by bus from station. Tel: 052 935 6262. Open: 10am–5pm; closed Monday. Admission charge.*

Nara

*T*he small town of Nara saw the first brilliant flowering of Japanese culture in the 8th century. Today it is a pleasant place set amid lush countryside, given over almost entirely to the celebration of its history. Much of the town is parkland, where deer roam freely (and appear in the most unexpected places).

Initially the Japanese moved their capital to a new site whenever the emperor died, to avoid pollution by his death. Then, in the 8th century, as their society became more complex, they planned a great and permanent capital. The site they chose was Nara, and the city was founded in 710. It was built on a grid plan, like the capital of neighbouring China, its splendid white-walled buildings embellished with vermilion pillars and green-tiled roofs.

In the new capital culture and the arts

flourished, underpinned by Buddhist faith. The culmination was the building of Todaiji with its colossal Great Buddha, the largest bronze image in the world. When the image was unveiled, foreign potentates from along the Silk Road came bearing gifts to attend the ceremony.

But in 784 the powerful Fujiwara family, who dominated Japan, decided to move the capital again – briefly to Nagaoka and then to Kyoto. Nara was left outside the mainstream of history; as

NARA TOWN PLAN

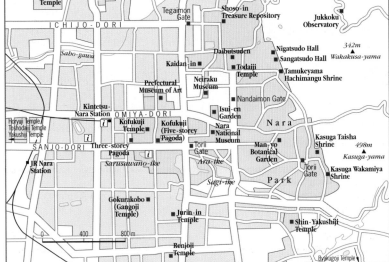

The graceful pagoda of Kofukuji Temple, set in Nara Deer Park

a result, while Kyoto burnt down again and again, several of Nara's temples and works of art – the legacy of a mere 74 years as capital – have survived for over 1,200 years, testimony to the glory of this ancient capital.

Nara is small enough to cover on foot; or you can rent a bicycle. The main sights are fairly close together in and near the deer park.

30 minutes–1 hour from Kyoto by train, via Uji.

Information: Nara City Tourist Centre, tel: 0742 22 3900; also in Nara and Kintetsu Nara stations.

KASUGA TAISHA SHRINE

A multitude of stone lanterns (1,780 in all) line the steps leading up to the grand vermilion halls of Kasuga Taisha Shrine. This famous shrine was founded in the 8th century by the immensely powerful Fujiwara family to be the guardian shrine of the new capital. Until the middle of the 19th century it was rebuilt every 20 years, according to Shinto custom (see Ise, page 99). The present buildings (1863) still faithfully follow the Heian style. The shrine is famous for performances of sacred dance. The treasure-house contains masks and drums used in dancing, and other ritual objects.

In the deer park. Shrine always open. Admission free. Treasure-house open daily, 8.30am–4.30pm April to October, 9am–4pm in winter. Admission charge.

KOFUKUJI

Kofukuji's five-storey pagoda is the symbol of Nara. Founded in the 8th century along with Kasuga Shrine, Kofukuji was the Fujiwara family temple and guardian temple of the capital. Not one of the original 175 buildings remains, all having been burnt to the ground; the buildings seen today are all later reconstructions. The five-storey pagoda dates from 1426 and the nearby three-storey pagoda from 1143. Several of the halls can be entered. To see Kofukuji's beautiful Buddhist sculptures, you will have to visit the treasure-house.

Central Nara. Grounds always open. Admission free. Treasure-house open: daily, 9am–5pm. Admission charge.

NARA KOKURITSU HAKUBUTSUKAN (Nara National Museum)

The Nara Museum has a fine collection of works of art produced during the first

flowering of Buddhism in Japan. The displays are organised according to the different Buddhist schools and include sculptures, calligraphy and paintings. The most priceless treasures are kept in the Shoso-in, a repository within the grounds of Todaiji (see opposite), with temperature and humidity carefully regulated to preserve the 1,200-year-old objects. These are the gifts brought from as far afield as ancient Persia to Emperor Shomu on the founding of Todaiji, and include Silk Road ceramics, textiles and glassware. Usually the treasures are not on view, but once a year, for two weeks in late October and early November, some are displayed in the Nara Museum; at that time the grounds of the Shoso-in are also open.

50 Noborioji-cho, just beyond Kofukuji. Tel: 0742 22 7771. Open: 9am–4.30pm (enter by 4pm); closed Monday. Admission charge.

SHIN-YAKUSHIJI

Down a quiet street to the south of the deer park, with pleasant views across the surrounding hills, is ancient Shin-yakushiji. Founded in 747 by Empress

Todaiji Temple, a great engineering achievement, houses Nara's 8th-century Great Buddha

Komyo to ensure her husband's recovery from illness, the 8th-century main temple building survives. It houses a wooden image of the Buddha of Healing, surrounded by 12 splendid Divine Generals.
Just outside deer park, near Kasuga Shrine. Open: daily, 8.30am–6pm, 8.30am–5.30pm in winter. Admission charge.

TODAIJI
Nara's Great Buddha is one of the most famous and important sights in Japan. The temple which houses the image, the 'Eastern Temple', is the largest wooden structure in the world, at 48m high a notable feat of engineering.

After several attempts, the Great Buddha was successfully cast in 745. It represented the apogee of the glorious culture of the Nara court and was unveiled with great ritual and ceremonial in 752. The image is of Vairocana Buddha, the essential Buddha, of whom all others are aspects. In the grounds is the Ordination Hall, which contains four famous 8th-century clay images of the guardians of the four directions.
Within deer park. Open: daily, 7.30am–5.30pm April to September, 7.30am–5pm October, 8am–4.30pm November to February, 8am–5pm March. Admission charge.

Nara Environs

*M*oving south from Nara you travel ever further back in time, to the very beginnings of Japanese civilisation at Asuka (see page 118). The high point of any exploration of the Nara environs is undoubtedly the ancient temple complex at Horyuji. Much is made of the fact that Horyuji is the world's oldest wooden structure. What is said less often is that it provides a rare chance to breathe the air of a long-vanished world.

HORYUJI

In a small town a few kilometres southwest of Nara is a complex of temples and pagodas which have stood for nearly 1,400 years. Horyuji was founded in 607 by Shotoku Taishi (Prince Shotoku), the greatest figure in ancient Japanese history. A philosopher prince, he melded the Japanese people into one, under the rule of the emperor, and made Buddhism the national religion. Under his guiding hand Japan developed a culture that rivalled China's. The pinnacle of his work was Horyuji.

What we see today at Horyuji is ancient weathered buildings, perfectly proportioned, which would have been brilliantly painted in Prince Shotoku's time, the orange pillars, white walls and green shutters designed to dazzle visiting envoys from China and Korea.

The buildings of the Western Precinct house ancient and beautiful images, in style close to the Buddhist art found along the Silk Road. There are serene bronze Buddhas, their eyes closed in meditative bliss, and exquisitely delicate paintings adorning the eaves of the main temple.

Within the treasure-house are objects which give some idea of the opulence of aristocratic life in those days. Look in particular for the Tamamushi Tabernacle, an altar which belonged to an empress and was originally entirely covered in the iridescent wings of millions of *tamamushi* jewel beetles (sadly, the wings have long since rotted away).

Lastly you reach the Hall of Dreams, built to appease Prince Shotoku's soul after his death. Within this elegant octagonal building is the Hidden Statue, a lifesize image of Prince Shotoku, worshipped as the Kuse Kannon, the Buddhist Saviour. Protected within its shrine for many centuries, the statue is perfectly preserved. Even now it is hidden for most of the time, only on view annually between 11 April and 5 May and 22 October and 3 November .
10 minutes from Nara by train and bus. Tel: 07457 4 2276. Open: daily, 8am–5pm 11 March to 19 November; 8am–4.20pm in winter (last entry 1 hour before closing). Admission charge.

TOSHODAIJI

This beautiful monastery complex was founded in 759 by the Chinese priest Ganjin, who had been invited to Japan by the emperor to tighten up monastic training. Many of the original buildings still stand, including the graceful Main Hall, with its unusual rounded pillars. The hall contains a striking image of Vairocana, the Cosmic Buddha, with a thousand tiny Buddhas forming the halo. There is also a wonderful lacquered statue of the blind old priest Ganjin

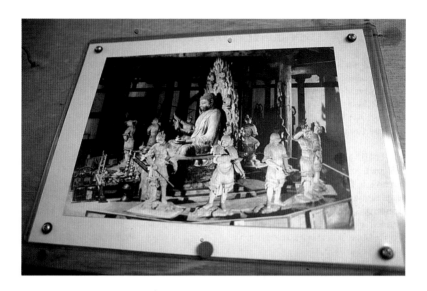

Statues pictured in the hall of Yakushiji Temple; and (below) a guardian deity at Horyuji

himself in the Miei-do Hall.
5 minutes' walk from Nishinokyo station,
15 minutes south of Nara by train. Open:
daily, 8.30am–4.30pm (last entry 4pm).
Admission charge.

YAKUSHIJI

Yakushiji was founded a few decades
after Horyuji, in 680. The only original
building is the graceful East Pagoda; the
West Pagoda and Main Hall are recent
reconstructions, as faithful as possible to
the originals and painted in the same
brilliant vermilion, white and green.
Yakushiji contains some of the finest and
most famous works of the period,
notably the Yakushi Trinity – statues of
the Lord of the Eastern Paradise and his
two attendants.
Close to Nishikyo station, 10 minutes from
Toshodaiji. Open: daily, 8.30am–5pm.
Admission charge.

NOTO HANTO (Noto Peninsula)

Noto, the small peninsula shaped like a crooked finger which juts into the Japan Sea north of Kanazawa, is famous for its remote and unspoilt beauty. Here terraced paddy fields stretch down to the sea and local fishermen hang out their nets to dry. Nowadays there are good roads and summer visitors come to fish and swim; but seconds away from the road the pace of life is as slow as ever. The centre of the area is the fishing port of Wajima. Here, you can visit the outdoor market where local women sell fish and vegetables, buy the peninsula's famous lacquerware and watch a performance of demon drumming by masked dancers.

Use car or bicycle. 2 hours by bus, 2½ hours by train from Kanazawa via Wajima.

OBUSE

For lovers of *ukiyo-e* woodblock prints and devotees of the master artist Hokusai, Obuse is worth a visit. When Hokusai was an old man, one of the merchants here became his patron and Obuse has a collection of some of his best late works – depictions of elephants, tigers, *ukiyo-e* beauties and Mount Fuji with a dragon issuing from its mouth.

20 minutes from Nagano by train. Hokusai-kan. Tel: 0262 47 5206. Open: daily, 9am–5pm April to October, 9.30am–4.30pm in winter. Admission charge.

OSAKA

According to Japanese lore, when Osakans meet they don't ask: 'How are you?' but rather 'Making any money?' . Founded by the great warlord Hideyoshi Toyotomi in the 16th century, Osaka was and is a city of merchants. Today it is Japan's third largest city. Much of the country's industrial output is produced here, including textiles, pharmaceuticals, iron and steel, and 40 per cent of exports pass through Osaka's airport and docks.

Osaka used to be a city of concrete, but in recent years it has become more pleasant: trees line its boulevards and parks are being laid out. There are a few

Above and below left: in its heyday, Osaka Castle was the most formidable fortress in the land

historical sights, notably Hideyoshi's fortress, Osaka Castle, once a fortified city. The present castle is a reconstruction, but still worth seeing. Sumiyoshi Shrine in the south of the city, founded in the 4th or 5th century, has a beautiful arched bridge. Shitennoji was founded in 593; only Asuka Temple (see page 119) is older.

However, the essence of Osaka is not in its past but in its bustling streets, dazzling neon nightscapes and extraordinary modern architecture. The north of the city, centring around Osaka station, is more refined. Here, look out for the new Shin-Umeda Building, in a complex which includes the glamorous new Westin Hotel. As you move south, the lights grow brighter and the designs wilder. Be sure not to miss the Shinsaibashi/Dotombori area by night, where giant crabs, lobsters and dragons wave claws along the neon-lit streets and the wonderful Kirin Plaza (see page 33)

glows like a surreal lantern. Forget good and bad taste and enjoy the Japanese at play.
45 minutes from Kansai International Airport, 2½ hours from Tokyo by train.

SHIRAKAWA AND GOKAYAMA

In the narrow valleys between the mountains of Central Japan, the villagers of Shirakawa and Gokayama built *gassho-zukuri* houses. These enormous wooden farmhouses have huge smoke-darkened rafters and steeply sloping thatched roofs, like two hands pressed together in prayer (*gassho*). Many are now inns where visitors can experience the lifestyle of these country areas. In Shirakawa there is a folkcraft museum, a temple and fine mountain views. The villages of Gokayama are scattered along a spectacular gorge; the prettiest is Ainokura, nearest to Kanazawa.
2½ hours from Takayama, 2 hours from Kanazawa by infrequent bus.

Top: the mountain city of Takayama is famous for its steep-roofed houses, built to resist snow
Above: mothers whose children have died pray to jizo-sama images

TAKAYAMA

Surrounded by spectacular mountain ranges and in the past often cut off by snow, Takayama developed a robust and distinctive culture. Visitors come to stroll through the streets of splendid wooden houses, buy Takayama's woodcrafts, and taste the mountain cuisine. The best way to explore the town is by bicycle.

Asa-ichi (morning market)

In the morning, farmers bring vegetables, *miso* (soybean paste) and handicrafts and spread them along the riverside to sell. It's a lively scene, and you can indulge in some haggling.

Hida minzoku mura (Hida Folk Village)

Hida Folk Village is full of the nostalgic smell of woodsmoke. This famous open-air museum consists of 30 of the finest old farmhouses from the mountains around Takayama, lovingly reassembled. The buildings, of smoke-blackened wood with huge beams and thickly thatched roofs, were made in the traditional way, without nails.

5 minutes by bus south of station. Tel: 0577 33 4714. Open: daily, 8.30am–5pm. Admission charge.

Kusakabe mingeikan (Kusakabe folk museum)

This splendid house was built by the Kusakabe family in 1879 when, after years of repression, merchants were finally able to display their wealth. Made of the finest timbers, it is striking for its sheer size and lofty ceilings criss-crossed by enormous beams. Next door is Yoshijima ke (Yoshijima house), an elegant merchant's house of 1908.

20 minutes' walk north of station. Kusakabe mingeikan open: daily, 9am–5pm April to November, 9am–4.30pm in winter. Yoshijima ke open: 9am–5pm March to November, 9am–4.30pm in winter; closed Tuesday. Admission charge to each.

San-machi suji (San-machi street)

San-machi suji is the merchants' quarter and the heart of the old town. The narrow streets are lined with picturesque shops, restaurants, inns and *sake* breweries, the latter marked by a ball of cryptomeria leaves.

Across the red bridge from Takayama Jinya.

Takayama Jinya (Takayama government office)

Built as the palace of the local *daimyo*, this splendid building was taken over by the officers of the shogun in 1692 to use as the provincial government offices. There is a memorable torture chamber

with instruments of torture and vivid depictions of how they were used. Next to the main building is an enormous storehouse, the oldest extant, where sacks of rice, sent as taxes to the shogun, were stored.

10 minutes' walk from station. Open: daily, 8.45am–5pm April to October, 8.45am–4.30pm in winter. Admission charge.

Takayama is 2¼ hours from Nagoya by train. Tourist information office and bicycle rental at station.

TOBA

Toba is the home of Pearl Island, where Kokichi Mikimoto first succeeded in producing a cultured pearl. There is a pearl museum here, and you can also watch *ama*, women divers who dive supposedly for pearls (in fact they are diving for shellfish and seaweed). The surrounding area is very picturesque.

15 minutes from Ise, 1¼ hours from Nagoya by train.

YOSHINO

This mountain, deep in the heart of the central Japanese peninsula, has long been a place of retreat. Mountain priests carried out ascetic practices and emperors and lords fled here from their enemies. Today Yoshino is famous for its cherry blossom. In April the entire mountain is carpeted with pale pink blossom and the narrow village street is jam-packed. For the rest of the year it is quiet. People come to visit the temple of Kimpusenji and to climb through the village to the mountaintop shrine of Kimpu-jinja.

1¼ hours south of Osaka by train, then cable car. Kimpusenji open: daily 9am–5pm. Admission free. Kimpu-jinja always open. Admission free.

The Nakasendo 'Mountain Road'

This 7km hike takes you along a section of the old Nakasendo Highway, which used to run from Kyoto to Tokyo, through the mountain country of central Japan. The walk begins and ends at wonderfully preserved old post towns, which sprang up along the highway to cater to travellers. *Allow 4 hours.*

From Nakatsugawa, 1 hour northeast of Nagoya by train, take a bus to Magome (35 minutes).

1 MAGOME

Magome is a picturesque little town which straggles steeply up the hill along the old Nakasendo highway. Post towns were always long and narrow, lining the highway on both sides with inns, restaurants, tearooms and pleasure houses where weary travellers could relax. Magome is one of the very few post towns to remain much as it was. The shuttered wooden buildings, waterwheels and cobbled street have been carefully preserved. There are few electric cables visible and no cars, though souvenir shops have now replaced pleasure houses. As you climb the hill you will pass a museum dedicated to the town's most famous son, the novelist Shimazaki Toson (1872–1943).

At the road, walk or take a bus to Magome Pass. The path is clear and well signposted. Look for signs to Tsumago-juku in English.

2 MAGOME-TOGE (Magome Pass)

At Magome Pass, 801m above sea-level, there is a teashop and views across the surrounding mountains. From here, take the stony path which leads to the right of the teahouse steeply

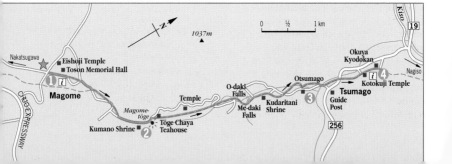

down into forest. At the time of the shoguns, there were only two highways linking Tokyo and Kyoto: the Tokaido, which went along the coast, skirting Mount Fuji, and the Nakasendo. People walked or travelled by palanquin or on horseback; wheeled traffic was forbidden. Along the way you pass a checkpoint, where guards were posted to prevent timber smuggling.

Follow the path out of the forest through a small village to a bridge. On the other side is the village of Otsumago.

3 OTSUMAGO

Otsumago's handsome old farmhouses still provide accommodation to passing travellers. Even if you don't stay, you can admire the dark wooden shutters and heavy overhanging eaves. There is also a working waterwheel.

Follow the path downhill to Tsumago. From Magome Pass the walk takes about 2 hours.

4 TSUMAGO

Tsumago is the most picturesque and perfectly preserved of the old post towns. You can stroll the cobbled street, stay in one of the romantic old inns which have welcomed travellers for centuries, and try mountain vegetables, *soba* buckwheat noodles and *gohei mochi* – rice cakes threaded on skewers and dressed with a nutty paste. The street is lined with dark wooden houses, pressed close together, with shop signs hanging outside; many sell local handicrafts. There is also an atmospheric old shrine, the village temple (up some stone steps), and the

Straw raincoats on sale in Tsumago, one of the finest of the highway's old post towns

house of the village magnate, made of fine local timber, now a folk museum (Okuya Kyodokan).

From Tsumago, the Nakasendo winds off invitingly to Nagiso, where you can take a train to Nagoya or Matsumoto. The walk takes 2 hours. Alternatively, you can take a bus, which takes 7 minutes.

Shimazaki Toson Museum – open: Friday to Monday, 8am–5pm. Admission charge.
Okuya Kyodokan – tel: 0264 57 3322. Open: daily, 8.30am–5pm. Admission charge.

The Asuka Plain

This cycle ride in search of traces of the earliest Japanese civilisation takes you through lush countryside of swaying bamboo groves, gently rolling hills and terraced paddy fields. *Allow 3–4 hours.*

Take the train to Asuka, 1 hour south of Nara, via Kashihara jingu-mae; also accessible from Osaka and Kyoto. At Asuka station, rent a bicycle. Cross the main road and follow the cycling track off to your left; watch for signposts in English to Takamatsuzaka tumulus.

1 TAKAMATSUZAKA KOFUN (Takamatsuzaka Tumulus)

The ride from Asuka station takes you through a serene, ageless landscape. Tucked into the hillside is the Takamatsuzaka Barrow Mural Museum; the tumulus itself is a few steps further on. When the tumulus was excavated in 1972, archaeologists found a chamber painted with astonishingly delicate and beautiful 7th-century frescos akin to Tang Chinese painting – people in court costume, a dragon, a tiger and a tortoise with a snake coiled around it. The tumulus is now sealed to preserve the frescos, but you can see perfect full-scale reproductions in the museum.

Return to main road; take cycling path which runs beside it. Watch for signposts in English for Ishibutai.

2 ISHIBUTAI

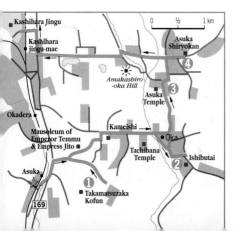

To your left you pass a large tumulus, the mausoleum of Emperor Temmu and Empress Jito. Cycle on and look for signs to Kameishi, an enormous rock carved with the face of a tortoise. On your right you pass Tachibana Temple, said to be the birthplace of Prince Shotoku (see page 110). Finally, at the top of a long incline, you come to Ishibutai ('stone stage'), an enormous 7th-century barrow, as big as a house, roofed with vast flat stones and surrounded by a dry moat. You can walk inside.

Ishibutai, an ancient burial mound, where Emperor Temmu and Empress Jito are laid to rest

Cycle back down the hill and follow signs to Asuka Temple; or study the maps that dot the area and take one of the cycling paths that wind through the hills to the temple.

3 ASUKA TEMPLE

Asuka Temple houses the oldest bronze Buddha in Japan, a large, serene image dating from 607. It has been through many fires and only the face and hands are original. The temple was founded in 588 and is the oldest in Japan. Behind it is a small stone pagoda.

Turn left out of temple. At the main road turn right and cycle up to Asuka Museum.

4 ASUKA SHIRYOKAN (Asuka Museum)

In the garden is a fountain made of two grotesque embracing figures, representative of the many strange stone figures which dot the area. Inside is a detailed exhibition of the many discoveries which have cast light on the highly advanced culture which developed in this area in the 7th century. Look in particular at the water-clock, perpetually

filling and emptying to indicate the passage of time. The exhibition is continually updated as excavations reveal new information.

Cycle back down the hill to Kashihara Jingu (Kashihara Shrine), dedicated to Japan's first emperor, Jimmu. Return your bicycle at Kashihara Jingu-mae station, from where there are trains to Osaka, Kyoto and Nara.

Takamatsuzaka Barrow Mural Museum – tel: 0744 54 3340. Open: 9am–5pm; closed Monday. Admission charge.
Ishibutai Barrow – open: 9am–5pm; closed Monday. Admission charge.
Asuka Temple – open: daily, 8am–5.30pm April to September, 8am–5pm in winter. Admission charge.
Asuka Museum – open: 9am–4.30pm; closed Monday. Admission charge.
Asuka General Information Office, tel: 0744 54 3624.

Western Honshu and Shikoku

*W*estern Japan is an area of contrasts – mountains and sea, shadows and light. At its heart is the Setonaikai (Inland Sea), bounded by Honshu to the north and Shikoku to the south. Islands dot the sparkling water and boats ply to and fro. Ancient battles took place here, and from these shores envoys once sailed back and forth between Japan and mainland Asia.

North of the sea is San-yo ('the sunny side of the mountains'), bustling with life and action. The bullet train runs along the coast and there is much heavy industry. But across the mountain ranges in San-in ('in the shadow of the mountains'), along the Japan Sea coast, life moves at a slower pace. The weather – cool and rainy – reflects the mood of this rural backwater.

Shikoku, the smallest of Japan's four main islands, is more remote still. Along the Inland Sea coast are busy ports. But travel inland and you find yourself among tangerine groves, terraced paddy fields and forested mountains, little changed over hundreds of years. Every

year many people make the pilgrimage around Shikoku's 88 temples, circling the island in the footsteps of Japan's greatest saint, Kobo Daishi (774–835), who was born here. Today Shikoku is more accessible than ever before, linked to the mainland by the new Seto Ohashi Bridge, the longest in the world, which carries road and rail traffic.

AMA-NO-HASHIDATE

This delicate sandspit, which is covered in gnarled pines, stretches across Miyazu Bay like the 'bridge of heaven' that is the meaning of its name, and is traditionally considered to be one of Japan's most beautiful sights. The recommended way to look at it is from Kasamatsu Park, on the other side of the bay, where you are supposed to bend over and admire the view from between your legs (from this rather ungainly position Ama-no-hashidate is said to

Dawn breaks over a glorious beach at the old fishing port of Hagi, centre of pottery and history

WESTERN HONSHU AND SHIKOKU

appear as if floating in mid-air).
San-in, 3 hours northwest of Kyoto by train.

FUKIYA

Situated in some of the most beautiful
mountain country in Japan, Fukiya was a
prosperous community a hundred years
ago, producing copper and red ochre
(used to stain woodwork). Wealthy mine-
owners commissioned splendid houses
before the copper ran out and Fukiya
turned into a ghost town. Today the old
houses are being restored and you can
visit the ochre mill and copper mine.
*San-yo, 2 hours northwest of Kurashiki, by
train and infrequent bus.*

HAGI

This gracious old fishing port is famous
for its lustrous rose-coloured pottery and
romantic history. From 1600 Hagi was
the domain of the Mori lords, opponents
of the shogun. In 1868, when the
shoguns were overthrown, fiery young
men from Hagi were at the forefront of
the rebellion. Japanese visitors still come
to pay their respects at the birthplaces
and graves of these heroes, and to
wander through the streets of samurai
houses.
*San-in, 2 hours from Kokura (Kita-
kyushu) by train; 1½ hours by express bus
from Ogori bullet train station.*

An artist tries to catch the essence of Japan's most beautiful castle – Himeji

HIMEJI

Its white turrets soaring above the plain like some great bird, Himeji Castle – 'the White Egret' – is indisputably Japan's most spectacular castle. Until the Meiji Restoration, it was a living, working castle, home to a succession of feudal lords and their innumerable retainers. You can climb the zigzag path to the castle entrance, its convoluted course providing the defenders with ample opportunity to bombard you from the many openings in the castle walls. If you have time for only one Japanese castle, this should be it.
San-yo, 30 minutes west of Osaka by train.

HIROSHIMA

Hiroshima would be no more than a large industrial city, with no particular interest, but for the dreadful event of 6 August 1945 when Hiroshima was the target for the world's first atomic bomb. The city has been rebuilt, but the A-Bomb Dome and Peace Park are eternal memorials.

Genbaku Domu (Atom Bomb Dome)

The Industrial Promotion Hall was almost exactly at the epicentre of the explosion. Its skeletal ruin is now the city's symbol.

Heiwa Kinen Koen (Peace Memorial Park)

The Peace Park contains memorials to the victims of the bomb and an eternal flame (to be extinguished when the last nuclear weapon has been destroyed). The Peace Memorial Museum in the park is a stark collection of items – the shadow of a man who had been standing outside a bank, watches fused at 8.15 – all the more moving for the simplicity of the presentation. A new wing explains the USA's decision to drop the bomb.
Peace Memorial Museum and Park open: daily, 9am–6pm May to November, 9am–5pm in winter. Admission charge.

San-yo, 4 hours west of Tokyo by bullet train. Information offices in station and Peace Memorial Park.

IMBE

The most sought-after pottery in Japan is *Bizen* ware, hand made with local clay and baked in wood-fired climbing kilns (many-chambered clay kilns built up the side of a hill). The pine ash used for firing gives a serendipitous natural glaze to the ware. The village of Imbe is the centre for *Bizen* ware, with many climbing kilns and a ceramics museum.
San-yo, 40 minutes east of Okayama by train. Bizen Togei bijutsukan (Ceramics Museum), tel: 0869 64 1400. Open: 9.30am–5pm, closed Monday. Admission charge.

IWAKUNI

An easy side trip from Miyajima or Hiroshima, Iwakuni is a placid town with a splendid bridge, Kintai-kyo (Brocade Sash Bridge), built in 1673 for samurai to strut across; *hoi polloi* had to cross by boat. Parts of the samurai quarter remain, together with a hilltop castle.

Hiroshima is a modern city, but the A-Bomb Dome still stands, a grim reminder of the recent past

San-yo, 20 minutes southwest of Hiroshima by train. Bridge: 15 minutes by bus from Shin-Iwakuni or Iwakuni station. Always open. Admission charge.

IZUMO

At the foot of steep, forested hills, in a magnificent natural setting, is Japan's oldest Shinto shrine, Izumo Taisha.

Dedicated to Okuninushi, deity of good fortune and marriage, it was originally raised high off the ground; the present main building dates from 1744. Worshippers invoke Okuninushi by clapping four times.

San-in, 30 minutes west of Matsue by train and bus. Also accessible by plane. Shrine always open. Admission free.

KOCHI

Cut off from the northern coast of Shikoku by near-impenetrable mountain ranges, the charming old city of Kochi has a Mediterranean flavour, with palm-lined streets, hot-blooded locals and a noisy morning market. It is famous for its fighting dogs, the Tosa mastiffs, who are ranked like sumo wrestlers. Kochi Castle, rebuilt 1753, was more of a residence than a castle, impossible to defend having living quarters on the ground floor opening on to the garden.

Shikoku, 2½ hours south of Okayama by train. Also accessible by plane. Castle open: daily, 9am–5pm, last entry 4.30pm. Admission charge.

KOTOHIRA

One of the best-loved pilgrimage places in Japan, Kotohira Shrine (1837) sprawls spectacularly across a mountainside. The main shrine is 800 steps up, in easy stages, with palanquins for the old or faint-hearted. Dedicated to the sun goddess Amaterasu, it is a wonderful, weatherbeaten building, ornately carved and thatched-roofed, with long verandas looking towards the Shikoku hills and across to the Inland Sea. The shrine is particularly venerated by seafarers, who have left offerings of model ships and old photographs of steamers.

Shikoku, 30 minutes southwest of Takamatsu or 1 hour south of Okayama by train.

KURASHIKI

In feudal times Kurashiki's excellent rice was stored in white-washed warehouses (*kura* means 'warehouse'), one of which was later used by industrialist local-boy-made-good Keisaburo Ohara to display his collection of western art. Today

Making contact: a child says hello to a statue of a dog in Kotohira shrine

---

LAFCADIO HEARN (1850–1904)
The English writer Lafcadio Hearn arrived in Matsue in 1890 and spent the rest of his life in Japan. He married a local girl and lived and dressed as a Japanese. He also took a Japanese name, Yakumo Koizumi, and became a naturalised Japanese citizen. From Matsue he moved to Kobe and later to Tokyo, but Matsue remained his first love. In his books, of which *Glimpses of Unfamiliar Japan* is the best known, he wrote of Japan and Japanese culture in page after page of purple prose. After his death he was honoured for his services to Japan.

Kurashiki is famous for its museums, and the canal area, lined with warehouses and willows, is a preservation zone. Besides the Ohara Museum, you can see the Mingeikan (Folk Art Museum), the Japanese Toy Museum, and many others.
San-yo, 15 minutes west of Okayama by train. Museums open: 9am–5pm, closed Monday. Admission charge for each.

Matsue Castle, in the city beloved of Lafcadio Hearn and now a magnet for his admirers

MATSUE

Lafcadio Hearn (see box opposite) dubbed Matsue 'The Chief City of the Province of the Gods' and immortalised it in his books. Today, Hearn's house has become a place of pilgrimage for his many Japanese readers. Matsue's black 17th-century castle is the city's other attraction, 'a vast and sinister shape, all iron-gray, rising against the sky from a cyclopean foundation of stone ...', as Hearn described it.
San-in, 2½ hours northwest of Okayama by train; or take a flight to Izumo or Yonago airport. Koizumi Yakumo Kyukyo (Lafcadio Hearn's House), tel: 0852 23 0714. Open: 9am–12.30pm, 1.30–4.30pm, closed Wednesday and 13 to 16 August. Admission charge. Matsue Castle, tel: 0852 21 4030. Open: daily, 8.30am–5pm. Admission charge.

PILGRIMAGE

If you visit temples and shrines in Japan, you are bound to come across busloads of rollicking pilgrims – a pilgrimage is much like a holiday. The streets leading to the most important shrines and temples are a perpetual carnival, bustling with people and lined with inns, teahouses, restaurants and souvenir shops selling religious mementoes. Pilgrims dress in white and carry staffs; even the frailest make it to the innermost shrine, often the top of a mountain.

Miyajima's magical *torii* gate, marking the approach to a sacred island

MIYAJIMA

Despite being one of the most famous places in Japan, Miyajima is truly magical. Visit in the evening when the crowds have gone and you have the place to yourself (along with the tame deer that roam the streets). Miyajima ('Shrine Island') was once so sacred that lay people were not permitted to step on its soil but approached by boat, via the huge *torii* which seems to float on the water. Wander round the island, explore the pagodas and temples, or ascend Mount Misen (on foot or by cable car) for a spectacular view over the Inland Sea.

San-yo, by train to Miyajima-guchi, 15 minutes west of Hiroshima; then ferry.

OKAYAMA

Okayama is a large city with several museums, a charming castle, and a garden officially rated one of Japan's three most beautiful.

Okayama Castle (1597, but reconstructed after World War II), nicknamed 'Crow Castle', is pitch-black. Korakuen is a perfect Japanese garden, a world in miniature, with hills, lakes, pavilions, even paddy fields and a tea plantation.

San-yo, 50 minutes west of Osaka by train; accessible by plane. Castle, 5 minutes east of station by tram. Tel: 086 225 2096. Open: daily, 9am–5pm. Admission charge. Korakuen, beside castle. Tel: 086 272 1148. Open: daily, 7.30am–6pm April to September, 8am–5pm in winter. Admission charge.

MATSUYAMA

High on a hill above the noise and bustle of the city, Matsuyama Castle with its turrets, donjon and massive stone walls evokes the samurai age. But what brings Japanese visitors here in their thousands is Dogo Onsen (Dogo Spa) with its famous thermal waters, good for stiff joints, digestion and nerves.

1 hour by hydrofoil from Hiroshima; 2¾ hours from Okayama by train; also acccessible by plane. Castle, 10 minutes from station by tram. Open: daily, 9am–5pm. Admission charge. Dogo Onsen, 20 minutes by tram from station. Open: daily, 6.30am–10pm. Admission charge.

TAKAMATSU

This lively port city at the southern end of Seto Ohashi Bridge is the main gateway to Shikoku from Honshu. Its chief glory is Ritsurin koen (Ritsurin Park), with manicured pine trees and lakes full of carp. Shikoku mura (Shikoku Village) is a collection of old thatched farmhouses from around the island, approached via a rickety vine bridge – not for the faint-hearted!

Shikoku, 1 hour from Okayama by train; or by plane or ferry. Ritsurin Park, 10 minutes by train south of station. Open: daily, sunrise to sunset. Admission charge. Shikoku mura, 15 minutes' walk from Yashima station. Tel: 0878 43 3111. Open: daily, 8.30am–5pm April–October, 8.30am–4.30pm in winter. Admission charge.

TOMO-NO-URA

On their way to Edo (Tokyo) to pay respects to the shoguns, Korean emissaries used to stay at Taichi-ro, the Wave-Facing Pavilion, in Tomo-no-ura. The view from there, they declared, was the loveliest in Japan. Not only the view –

of tiny exquisite islands, like an ink-brush painting – but the whole of this picturesque fishing port is a delight. Roam the narrow lanes, explore the castle ruins, or take a ferry out to the beaches on the islands.

San-yo, 30 minutes by bus from Fukuyama station.

TSUWANO

This pretty country town lies in a valley with steep hills rising to either side. High on one hillside are the ornate orange buildings of Taikodani Inari Shrine, reached through a tunnel of 2,000 *torii* or along a road blazoned with red banners. The ruins of Tsuwano Castle lie at the top of the ridge.

San-in, near Hagi; 1 hour by train from Ogori bullet train station; or 2 hours by steam train on summer Sundays (book in advance).

'Maple Leaf Valley' in Okayama's Korakuen Garden, one of the finest in the country

Cruising the Inland Sea

The Inland Sea (Setonaikai), with its misty islands rising poetically out of clear blue waters, is one of the most beautiful places in Japan. It has its quota of industries, particularly on the Honshu side, but you can still enjoy the unhurried pace of life on the islands. *Day trip.*

The easiest and most popular way to see the islands is aboard a Setonaikai (SKK) cruise, which goes from Miyajima to Onomichi, not far from Kurashiki. To book your ticket beforehand, telephone 082 253 1212. Alternatively use ferries to hop from island to island. Start from Miyajima or Hiroshima and buy a ticket initially for Omishima.

1 MIYAJIMA

The most enchanting place to begin your journey is at the ancient holy island of Miyajima (see page 126), one of the great sights of Japan. You set off, leaving its huge red *torii* behind you. There are said to be 3,000 islands in the Setonaikai (Inland Sea), most crowded into the stretch of water you are about to go through, and many have names and stories connected with them. Fishing boats and barges ply between fishing villages, past tiny craggy islands.

Pass through Ondo Straits, said to have been dug out by the warlord

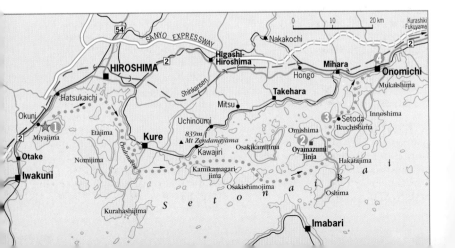

Miyajima's majestic *torii* is the first of many remarkable views along the Inland Sea cruise

Kiyomori Taira 800 years ago, and through a succession of small islands to reach Omishima.

2 OMISHIMA

Omishima is famous for its shrine, Oyamazumi Jinja, where the pirates who once controlled the Inland Sea used to worship. The shrine also has a treasure-house full of armour and weapons which belonged to great heroes from Japanese history. But rather than seeing these you may prefer to use the two-hour break in your tour to borrow a bicycle (rent free, at the pier). Cycle around the island on the well-marked cycling paths and savour the empty roads, orange groves, slate-roofed cottages and rugged forested hills.

From Omishima take the boat or a ferry to Setoda, the port on Ikuchishima island.

3 SETODA

The tourist attraction here is Kosanji, a bizarre construction erected by a local who made his fortune in the steel tube industry, and dedicated the temple to his mother. You may safely avoid this.

Instead, rent a bicycle at the pier and spend your free hour exploring the island. The port town of Setoda itself is full of charming old houses. Inland there is a large lake formed by a dam from where you can look back to the bay, full of cranes and fishing boats, and to the islands all around.

From Setoda, take the boat or a ferry on to Onomichi.

4 ONOMICHI

Onomichi, back on the Honshu mainland, is an interesting little town straggling along a hillside and overlooked by a tiny castle. Most of the streets are too steep and narrow for cars. Walk along the lanes, exploring the innumerable temples: the most notable are Senkoji, at the top of the hill, from where you can look down on the town and the sea, and Jodoji, which has a long history and some unusual buildings.

From Onomichi, the JR Sanyo Line has trains every 15 minutes east to Fukuyama, for Tomo-no-ura (see page 127), Okayama or Osaka, or west to Hiroshima.

The Tropical South

*I*f you are travelling by bullet train, your first view of Kyushu, the southern-most of Japan's four main islands, will be the smokestacks and shipyards of Kitakyushu. Kyushu has been dubbed Japan's Silicon Island; besides being home to the massive Nippon Steel Works, Kitakyushu is the country's centre for the manufacture of semi-conductors and IC chips.

Don't worry. Once clear of the northernmost strip, the south of Japan is idyllically beautiful. Japanese holidaymakers visit Kyushu for its panoramic views and dramatic live volcanoes. This is where the history of Japan, both legendary and factual, begins. It is said that when the wind god Ninigi came to rule Japan, he alighted on Mount Takachiho in the Kirishima

Okinawan women at the old capital, Shuri

range. And it seems likely that remote ancestors of the Japanese, among them the ancestors of the imperial family, migrated from Korea, on mainland Asia, across to Kyushu.

Okinawa, with its clear blue seas and silver beaches, is a paradise for watersports, with the best scuba diving in Asia. The people and culture are completely distinct from Japanese, and there are many traces of that ancient culture to be found.

TAKAMORI SAIGO (1827–77)
The great romantic hero of Japan's modern era was a hot-blooded Kyushu man. Takamori Saigo was a larger-than-life figure, a huge man with eyes that sparkled 'like black diamonds' and a great bull head. A poor samurai from the southern city of Kagoshima, he was a brilliant soldier, instrumental in bringing about the overthrow of the shogun and the Meiji Restoration of 1868. He became part of the new government, but quickly found himself opposed to his colleagues. He retreated to Kagoshima, from where, in 1877, he launched a rebellion. Thousands died, but the rebellion was doomed to failure, and on 23 September Saigo committed ritual suicide. His statue broods at the entrance to Tokyo's Ueno Park.

THE TROPICAL SOUTH

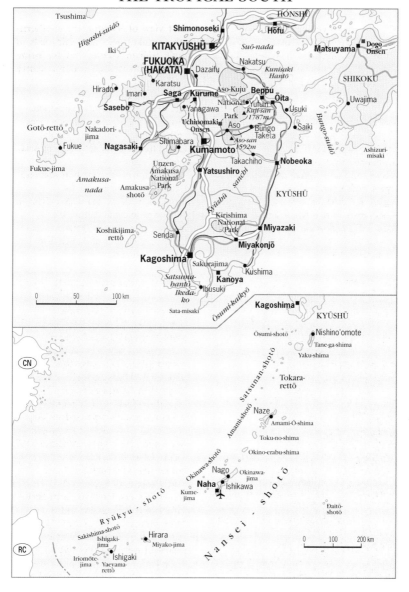

Posing for a photograph at the edge of the enormous crater of Mount Aso

ASO-KUJU NATIONAL PARK

Fifty thousand years ago, a series of huge explosions produced one of the largest calderas on earth. Within Mount Aso's vast outer rim, more than 20km across, are farms, villages and several smaller volcanoes. One at least is far from dormant. You can take the cable car or drive to the rim of Naka-dake and peer at the seething green lava in its depths.

It is worth stopping off at the nearby town of Bungo Taketa, to admire the romantic ruins of Oka Castle, perched high on the ridge.

Central Kyushu, 1 hour east of Kumamoto, 2 hours southwest of Beppu by train. Bus from station to cable car. Bungo Taketa lies between Aso and Beppu by train or bus.

BEPPU

Beppu is a large seaside city whose major industry is fun. It is crammed with hotels, neon signs, tour buses and a breathtaking variety of entertainments. For hot spring enthusiasts Beppu is paradise. There are 'hells', where steam and hot water gush from the rocks, and many different spas – outdoor pools, jungle baths and hot sands. There is even a sex museum. If nothing else, Beppu does provide an insight into the Japanese at play.

Northeast Kyushu, accessible by plane (Oita airport). 2½ hours southeast of Hakata and 3½ hours northeast of Kumamoto by train.

DAZAIFU

Once the ancient capital of Kyushu and southern outpost of the Nara government, Dazaifu is a place of pilgrimage for millions of students eager to pass their exams. Just beyond the station, shops selling calligraphy brushes line the entrance to Tenman-gu Shrine,

But primarily it is a sparkling modern city. The Tenjin area is where the young and chic go shopping; to see affluent modern Japan, visit the gold-plated IMS Building there. The Nakasu area, between Fukuoka's two rivers, comes alive in the evening, when everyone goes to eat, drink and be merry. Fukuoka also boasts Japan's largest disco; the 234m-high Fukuoka Tower incorporating 8,000 mirrors; and the country's most hi-tech baseball stadium, the Fukuoka Dome, opened in 1993 and home to the city's newest, proudest acquisition, the Daiei Hawks baseball team.

Northern Kyushu, 6½ hours west of Tokyo by train; also accessible by plane.
Information: Rainbow Plaza, IMS Building 8F. Tel: 092 733 2220.

Steam rises from one of Beppu's eight 'hells'

dedicated to Tenjin, god of poets and calligraphers. A historical figure, Tenjin was a 9th-century scholar named Sugawara no Michizane, who was exiled to Dazaifu and died there. Besides his shrine, the small town of Dazaifu has several important temples.

Northern Kyushu, 20 minutes southeast of Fukuoka by train.

FUKUOKA

Step off the bullet train at Fukuoka, and you could be in Tokyo. Fukuoka (confusingly, the station is called Hakata, after the old merchant quarter, while the city is called Fukuoka, after the samurai section) is no backwoods provincial city. It is far enough from Tokyo to have established itself as a capital in its own right – the capital of Silicon Island.

Fukuoka has its quota of historical sights, notably the 12th-century Shofukuji, Japan's oldest Zen temple.

Kagoshima and Environs

*E*ven on fine days there is always a faint pall of smoke over Kagoshima. Wherever you turn, you can't fail to notice the brooding cone of the volcano Sakurajima across the bay, trailing an ominous plume of smoke. Often umbrellas are up, as a drizzle of black ash rains down on the city.

For centuries the capital of the Shimazu clan, Kagoshima has a long, idiosyncratic history. St Francis Xavier landed here in 1549, determined to convert Japan to Christianity, while in the 19th century the fiery Shimazu clan led the rebellion to topple the shogun. Modern Kagoshima is a port and industrial city.

Iso Teien (Iso Garden)

The Shimazu lords built their villa against the spectacular backdrop of Sakurajima. You can stroll through the rooms, lined with gold leaf, where they entertained western potentates. In the grounds is a fascinating historical museum in Japan's first modern factory, established by the Shimazu.
10 minutes north of Kagoshima station by bus. Tel: 0992 47 1551. Open: daily, 8.30am–5.30pm March–October, 8.30am–5pm in winter. Admission charge.

Kagoshima's tropical flowers in bloom

Sakurajima

The most exciting thing to do in Kagoshima is to take the ferry across to Sakurajima. An extremely lively volcano, Sakurajima has small eruptions every day. One huge explosion in 1914 produced enough lava to join the island to the mainland, while another buried several villages. The most recent big eruption was in 1960. There are several look-out points around the island, with breathtaking views, and lava shelters in case of another eruption.
15 minutes from Sakurajima Pier by ferry; ferries operate 24 hours. There are buses around the volcano, or rent a bicycle.

Kagoshima is in southern Kyushu, 4 hours south of Hakata by train, also accessible by plane. Tourist information office: Nishi-Kagoshima station. Tel: 0992 53 2500.

KAGOSHIMA ENVIRONS

Kagoshima is the gateway to the Satsuma-hanto (Satsuma Peninsula) and some of Japan's most glorious tropical scenery. The journey down the coast takes you past white beaches, rocky outcrops, dense bamboo groves and hillsides covered in tea plantations or terraced paddy fields. At the tip of the peninsula are Lake Ikeda, a serene caldera lake where giant eels reside, and the picture-book perfect cone of Mount Kaimon.

The smoking cone of Sakurajima, seen from the ferry on its way back to Kagoshima

Chiran

In this charming small town, a whole street of samurai houses is preserved. Each has a garden using rocks, stone lanterns, hedges and raked gravel to create a landscape in miniature.

Chiran was one of the bases from which the *kamikaze* pilots took off in the last desperate months of World War II. The Tokko Heiwa Kaikan (Peace Museum for Kamikaze Pilots) is a collection of memorabilia – letters, photographs, aeroplanes – of the youths who died.

1¼ hours by bus south of Kagoshima. Samurai street open: daily, 8am–5.30pm. Admission charge. Tokko Heiwa Kaikan (tel: 0993 83 2525) open: daily, 9am–5pm. Admission charge.

Ibusuki

A pleasant seaside town, Ibusuki offers two extraordinary experiences. One is being buried up to your neck in steaming hot sand. The other is the Jungle Bath, where you bathe in a variety of pools surrounded by tropical foliage. For hot spring connoisseurs, it is unmissable. There is also a museum of modern art, the Iwasaki Bijutsukan, in a building designed by one of Japan's leading architects, Fumihiko Maki.

1 hour south of Kagoshima by train. Sunamushi-buro (sand bath), on the beach, 20 minutes' walk from station. Open: daily, 8.30am–8.30pm. Jungle Bath, in Kanko Hotel. Open: daily, 7am–10pm. Iwasaki Bijutsukan, next to Kanko Hotel. Open: daily, 8am–5.30pm. Admission charge to all.

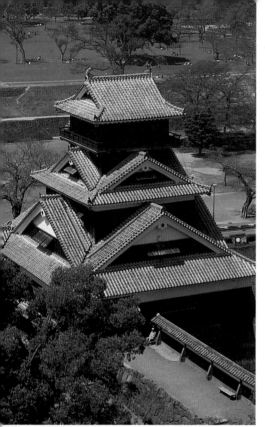

A corner turret of Kumamoto's massive castle, rebuilt after the original was destroyed by fire

producer of microchips, as its main employer. The city's magnificent castle burnt down in 1877 while under siege by Takamori Saigo (see page 130). It was rebuilt and houses a fascinating collection of treasures of the Hosokawa clan, the long-time rulers of the area. Kumamoto's elaborate landscaped garden, Suizenji Koen (Suizenji Park), features a miniature Mount Fuji covered in grass as the focal point of interest.

Western Kyushu, accessible by plane; 1½ hours south of Fukuoka by train. Kumamoto Castle, 15 minutes by tram from station. Open: daily, 8.30am–5.30pm April to October, 8.30am–4.30pm in winter. Admission charge. Suizenji Park, 30 minutes by tram from station. Open: daily, 7.30am–6pm, 7.30am–5pm in winter. Admission charge.

KIRISHIMA NATIONAL PARK

The peaks of the Kirishima range rise out of lush tropical countryside. According to ancient creation myths, this is where the wind god Ninigi alighted when he came down to rule earth. His halberd is still there, embedded on the top of Mount Takachiho. A spectacular day-long walk will take you across five peaks to Takachiho's vast bowl-shaped crater.

Southern Kyushu, 2 hours by train and bus north of Kagoshima.

KUMAMOTO

Kumamoto is a large, energetic, modern city, with NEC, the world's largest

KUNISAKI HANTO (Kunisaki Peninsula)

One of the most isolated and remote corners of Japan, Kunisaki has steep wooded hills, with tiny villages tucked into the valleys or high on the hillsides. A Buddhist stronghold in ancient times, it is rich in stone images and ancient temples.

Northeastern Kyushu, accessible by plane (Oita airport), car or bus tour from Beppu.

NAGASAKI

Nagasaki hit world headlines on 9 August 1945, when the second atomic bomb laid it waste and ended World War II. Before that this picturesque port city, straggling up the hillsides around

Nagasaki Bay, had a long history of contact with the west, and its streets and old buildings tell the story of its fascinating past.

Dejima
For some 220 years from 1639, Japan's only window to the west was the Dutch trading post on the island of Dejima.
En route to Graba-en by tram.

Graba-en (Glover Garden)
In the Meiji period, European merchants lived in Nagasaki in colonial splendour. One such was the Scotsman Thomas Glover (1838–1911), who supplied arms to the rebels opposing the shogun, helped build Japan's first railway and married a geisha. His house and those of other merchants are in this park.
Graba-en, 10 minutes by tram south of station. Open: daily, 8am–6pm, March to November, 8.30am–5pm in winter. Admission charge.

Heiwa Koen (Peace Park)
The second atomic bomb fell on a heavily populated working-class area, killing 150,000 people. The peace museum, renovated for the 50th anniversary of the ending of the war, contains a simple and shocking collection of relics, with material on Japan's war role.
Nagasaki kokusai bunka kaikan (International Culture Hall), 10 minutes by tram north of station. Tel: 0958 44 1231. Open: daily, 8.30am–5.30pm. Admission charge.

Koushi-byo (Confucian Shrine and Museum of Chinese History)
The Confucian shrine is a glorious building with a brilliant yellow roof made of Beijing tiles. The museum contains artefacts from the Beijing National Museum.
Next to Graba-en. Tel: 0958 24 4022. Open: daily, 8.30am–5pm. Admission charge.

Sofukuji
Nagasaki's temple area is well worth exploring. Sofukuji, founded by Chinese residents in 1629, has a wonderful Ming-dynasty gateway.
Behind Koushi-byo. Open: daily, 8am–5pm. Admission charge.

Nagasaki is in western Kyushu. Accessible by plane; 2 hours by train south of Fukuoka. Tourist information office, in station. Tel: 0958 23 3631.

Guarding the magnificent Ming dynasty gateway at Sofukuji Temple in Nagasaki

THE CLOSED SOCIETY

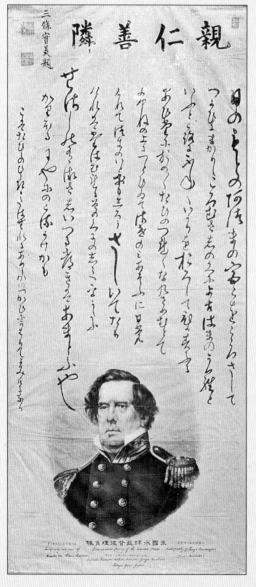

三條實美題

隣善仁親

米國水師提督波音假像

In 1543 a group of Portuguese sailors, blown off course, landed on the island of Tanegashima, near Nagasaki. These were the first westerners to arrive in Japan, and they were quickly followed by others. The Japanese called the new arrivals *namban*, 'southern barbarians', and Nagasaki became the centre for a huge boom in all things Portuguese. Debonair Japanese youths swaggered the streets dressed in ruffs, capes and pantaloons.

Then came a reversal of fortune. In 1600 Ieyasu Tokugawa became shogun of a newly unified Japan. Convinced that the foreigners were a dangerous influence, he banned Christianity and sealed off the country. Not only could no foreigner enter, but no Japanese was allowed to leave; any who did leave and tried to return were executed. The only remaining Europeans were a few Dutch merchants, who were permitted to maintain a small trading post on Dejima (see page 137).

For 220 years Japan remained closed, but Dejima was a peephole through

which the Japanese kept an eye on the astonishing changes taking place in the world outside.

In 1853 the American Commodore Matthew C Perry steamed into Tokyo Bay and demanded that Japan open up to trade with the west. The Japanese did not have the military strength to resist. In the upheavals that followed, the shogun was overthrown. The leaders of the rebellion, young samurai from Kagoshima (see page 134) and Hagi (see page 121), established the country's first modern government, with the Emperor Meiji as titular head.

Japan leapt into the modern age with dazzling speed. Within a few years

Opposite page: Commodore Matthew Perry
Above: Perry meets the Imperial Commission; cannon at Dejima; Glover Mansion, Nagasaki

of the emperor moving his capital from Kyoto to Tokyo, Japan had lighthouses, telephones and western education and legal systems. The first railway, linking Tokyo and Yokohama, opened in 1873, with the emperor and his entourage riding on the first train.

The Ryukyu Islands

*T*he Ryukyus are more like a South Sea paradise than a part of Japan. This chain of tiny islands, with lush palm groves, white beaches and brilliant blue seas, stretches for nearly 1,000km between the southernmost tip of Kyushu and Taiwan in the East China Sea. Most of the archipelago comes under the Japanese prefecture of Okinawa.

For centuries Okinawa was an independent kingdom, with its capital at Shuri (on the island of Okinawa) and a fascinating culture. It has had a long and troubled relationship with Japan. Despite terrible destruction during World War II, some of its distinctive and colourful architecture, music, art and crafts remain. Okinawa's sultry climate and languid lifestyle make it the most exotic place you will visit in Japan. But go soon – the region is fast being turned into a theme park for Japanese holidaymakers.

IRIOMOTE-JIMA

Iriomote is Japan's last frontier. Blanketed in dense tropical rainforest, it offers wonderful hiking, a river trip up a mini-Amazon, and some of the best scuba diving in Asia. Divers come specially to see the giant manta rays. If you are lucky you may also spot the extremely rare Okinawan wildcat.
1 hour by ferry southwest of Ishigaki.

ISHIGAKI-JIMA

Ishigaki is the gateway to the most distant and remote of the Ryukyu Islands – the Yaeyamas, which include Taketomi and Iriomote. It has tropical scenery, glorious beaches and fine diving.
Accessible by plane or 20 hours by ferry southwest of Naha.

KUME-JIMA

Much of Kume-jima is breathtakingly beautiful, with rows of sugarcane, Ryukyu pines and red-tiled roofs. The Uezu House, the oldest remaining traditional Okinawan house, belonged to the local lords and dates from 1726. Kume-jima is famous for its beautiful silk *pongee* fabrics.

*Accessible by plane or 3½ hours by ferry southwest of Naha.
Uezu House, Gushikawa Village, 5 minutes by bus from Nakadomari Town.
Open: daily, 8am–5pm.
Admission charge.*

A worker takes a break from chopping sugar cane, the main cash crop on Miyako-Jima

Glorious seascapes surround the Okinawan islands: this example is seen from Miyako-Jima

MIYAKO-JIMA

This idyllic island is the core of the Miyako group, eight islands between Okinawa and the Yaeyamas, with their own distinct culture. If you come during the low spring tides, you can see the huge Yaebishi reef emerging from the sea like a phantom island.

Accessible by plane or 10 hours by ferry southwest of Naha.

OKINAWA-JIMA

Any visit to the islands begins at Naha, the capital of Okinawa island, the largest and most important in the chain. A lively city with a tropical atmosphere, Naha is less frenetic and more relaxed than mainland Japan. Don't miss nearby Shuri, the capital of ancient Okinawa. The castle and great ceremonial gate (Shurei no Mon) are inevitably postwar reconstructions but, close to the originals, they communicate the exotic flavour of this once great kingdom. Outside Naha is fine countryside; the

north of the island is particularly unspoilt. Look for the castle ruins at Nakagusuku (1448), on a hilltop in central Okinawa, and Nakijin (14th century), on the Motobu peninsula.

Shuri, 25 minutes by bus from central Naha. Nakagusuku, 45 minutes by bus from Naha. Nakijin, 3½ hours by bus from Naha. Both open: daily, 9am–6pm, 9am–5.30pm in winter. Admission charge.

TAKETOMI-JIMA

This perfect, tiny island preserves much of the flavour of old Okinawa. Its single village is a cluster of houses, their red-tiled roofs topped with clay guardian lions to scare away evil spirits.

10 minutes by ferry from Ishigaki.

Naha is the transport hub for the whole surrounding area, accessible by plane and ferry from many Japanese cities and also from Taiwan. Okinawa Prefectural Tourist Federation, 306-1 Kagamimizu, Naha. Tel: 098 857 6884.

SAGA

The Saga area is home to three celebrated pottery towns. Karatsu produces elegant muted stoneware, while Imari and Arita make the country's most famous porcelain.

Northern Kyushu. 2–3 hours west of Fukuoka by train and bus.

TAKACHIHO

Takachiho is a small town set in lush countryside, where terraced paddy fields climb the foothills of craggy peaks. According to myth, the sun goddess once hid in a cave in one of its picturesque gorges. Nothing could persuade her to come out, until a young goddess performed an erotic dance which set the gods laughing so uproariously that the sun goddess peeped out – and the world was saved. The cave is still there, with an atmospheric old shrine above it. You can watch the nightly performance of sacred dance (Iwato Kagura) at Takachiho Jinja (Takachiho Shrine), culminating in an erotic dance as entertaining as the one which lured the sun goddess out.

Central Kyushu, 2 hours by bus southeast of Mount Aso. Iwato Kagura at Takachiho Jinja, nightly, 8–9pm. Admission charge.

USUKI

An interesting sidetrip from Beppu, Usuki is a small town with some of the finest and most ancient stone Buddhas in Japan.

Eastern Kyushu, 40 minutes by train south of Beppu. Usuki sekibutsu (stone Buddhas), 20 minutes by bus from station. Open: daily, 8.30am to sunset. Admission charge.

YANAGAWA

In the little town of Yanagawa ('Willow River'), the roads are intertwined with a network of moats and canals lined with willows. Boatmen in straw hats and *happi* coats punt you around the shallow reed-filled waterways.

Northern Kyushu, 1 hour south of Fukuoka by train.

YUFUIN

While its neighbour, the more famous Beppu (see page 132), is brash and neon-lit, Yufuin is a rustic retreat surrounded by mountains and swaying bamboo groves – in fact everything you ever imagined a Japanese spa to be.

Eastern Kyushu, 1 hour by bus from Beppu

Drying corn cobs, Takachiho

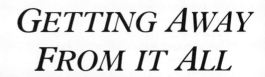

GETTING AWAY FROM IT ALL

'Over the wide plain the smoke-wreaths rise and rise,
Over the wide lake the gulls are on the wing;
A beautiful land it is, the Land of Yamato!'
EMPEROR JOMEI
(593–641)

Northern Escapes

*O*ne of Japan's best-kept secrets is its expanses of wild unspoilt country. Head away from the industrial heartland to the sparsely populated mountains of the north, where there are endless tracts of glorious alpine and volcanic scenery, with unlimited opportunities for walking, mountain-climbing, skiing or simply admiring the view. Northern roads tend to be fairly empty, except at the height of summer, so driving is a viable way of seeing the countryside.

For Japanese, a journey to the mountains invariably incorporates a visit to a hot spring. Japan being a volatile volcanic country, there is sulphurous hot water gushing out of the ground wherever you go. You will doubtless quickly pick up the Japanese habit of enjoying a long hot soak after a strenuous day's travelling or hiking.

HOKKAIDO
Akan National Park
Akan has three magical crater lakes. Lake Kussharo is vast and serene. Lake Mashu, deep and mysterious and rimmed by steep, forested slopes, was called the 'Lake of the Devil' by the Ainu. It is often obscured by cloud, but when visible is miraculously beautiful. Lake Akan was a centre for Ainu culture and is home to a mysterious green alga, the Marimo weed. There is little hiking in the area; all three lakes are accessible by bus or car. (See also page 60.)

Daisetsuzan National Park
Daisetsuzan is Japan's largest national park and a paradise for hikers. Most people begin their visit at Sounkyo Gorge, a dramatic ravine with plunging waterfalls and fantastically-shaped rocks. A road runs the length of the gorge, or you can rent a bicycle or walk. You can also begin the climb at the mountain spa of Asahidake. From here a cable car takes you up into another world, where alpine plants bloom against forbidding volcanic slopes. Hiking trails criss-cross the area. The seven-hour walk between Sounkyo and Asahidake follows a high windswept ridge, skirting the rims of several craters. (See also pages 60–1.)

A waterfall at the spectacular Sounkyo Gorge, in Daisetsuzan National Park

Rishiri-Rebun National Park

Hikers visit these northernmost islands of Hokkaido to trek to the summit of Rishiri, a spectacular volcanic cone rising straight out of the sea. You can also walk the length of Rebun, along clifftops and shingly beaches. In summer the islands are brilliant with wild flowers. (See also page 72.)

Shikotsu-Toya National Park

The most accessible of Hokkaido's national parks, Shikotsu-Toya centres around two beautiful crater lakes, Lake Toya and Lake Shikotsu. It has something for everyone – spectacular mountain scenery, hiking trails, volcanoes to climb and the region's most famous spa, Noboribetsu (see page 70). But what most visitors come to see are two very active volcanoes, Showa Shinzan, which thrust its way out of a farmer's field in 1943, and Mount Usu, which last erupted in 1977. (See also also page 71.)

Shiretoko National Park

Roads extend only part way along Shiretoko peninsula, in the far north of Hokkaido, and hikers who venture into the interior are warned to beware of bears. This is one area in Japan where bears still roam free; for the last 10 years they have been protected. The small town of Utoro, where explorations of the peninsula begin, is ugly but fun, full of

Autumn leaves provide a dramatic splash of colour at Akan National Park

Japanese who have fled from the rat race of Tokyo (see page 72).

TOHOKU

Most of Tohoku district is a gigantic national park, mile upon mile of rolling hills covered in impenetrable forest, interspersed with lakes, rivers and lush countryside carpeted with paddy fields. The Towada-Hachimantai national park, in the northern part of the region, is centred around two pleasant caldera lakes, Lake Towada and Lake Tazawa. (See also page 72.)

Sacred Mountains

Since ancient times the Japanese have believed that the gods live in beautiful natural surroundings – in particular on mountaintops. Traditionally, going on holiday meant a pilgrimage. This entailed making the climb, often long and dangerous, to the top of a sacred mountain to commune with the gods.

Today if you walk in the mountains in summer, you will find yourself in company with many white-clad pilgrims, wearing bells and carrying staffs. Along the way the paths are strewn with cairns, stone images and small shrines, while the summit of practically every mountain is crowned with a *torii* and shrine. The pilgrimage season and the popular time for climbing sacred mountains is July and August. In the winter the mountains are snowbound.

To the Japanese, the mountains are traditionally female and therefore jealous of other females. Until recently most

Yamabushi mountain priest, Dewa Sanzan

sacred mountains were closed to women; Mount Omine, the holiest of all, still is. The most famous sacred mountain is Mount Fuji (see pages 40 and 52–3). Other celebrated mountains include Takachiho, where the wind god Ninigi first alighted to rule earth (see page 136); Mount Koya, the headquarters of the esoteric Shingon Buddhist sect, 123 temples scattered across a wild mountaintop not far from Osaka (see page 104); and Mount Hiei, in Kyoto (see **Enryakuji**, page 78).

DEWA SANZAN (Three Mountains of Dewa)

Dewa Sanzan is one of Japan's most spectacular and famous sacred mountains and the headquarters of the mountaineering ascetics called *yamabushi*. The pilgrimage begins with the lowest of the three mountains that comprise Dewa Sanzan, Mount Haguro. You climb through ancient cryptomeria forests, up endless stone steps. The second mountain, Gassan ('Moon Mountain'), is a long hard trek across marshes and grass-covered slopes, with splendid views across the surrounding country. Finally pilgrims make the steep descent to Mount Yudono, to worship at the sacred hot spring there. Today, for pilgrims with less time, there is a bus to the summit of Haguro and another to Yudono. (See also page 61.)

OMINE-SAN (MOUNT OMINE)

There are two routes to Japan's most sacred mountain, Mount Omine. One begins at Kimpu-jinja (Kimpu Shrine) on the top of Mount Yoshino (see page 115), where a stone post proclaims in Japanese 'off limits to females'. The other begins at Kumano, the centre for the mountaineering priests of medieval times. From either direction it is a day-long hike to the

Above: inspecting a dragon pond on Mount Haguro, the lowest of Dewa's three mountains
Below: stone lions flanking the temple on Mount Haguro

top of Mount Omine. Pilgrims are expected to observe disciplines such as being hung by their heels over a cliff, to remind them of the frailty of their existence. For women, there are plenty of mountain walks skirting the forbidden Omine. (See also **Kii Peninsula**, page 103.)

OSORE-ZAN (Mount Osore)

Osore-zan means Terrible Mountain, and it is not difficult to believe, as many Japanese still do, that the souls of the dead gather there. It is a weird and desolate volcanic landscape of rocks, ash and rubble, where nothing grows and sulphur-laden steam stains the rocks yellow. The best time to visit is in July, during the four-day mediums' festival, the stars of which are blind women mediums. Japanese arrive in their thousands to commune with the souls of their dead. You can stay in the temple lodgings with the pilgrims and enjoy the very primitive mixed baths. (See also page 70.)

In the South

Japan's south is semi-tropical. Here life goes on at a different pace, amid the sultry heat and palm trees, often in the shadow of active volcanoes. The change begins just south of the industrial belt along the top of Kyushu.

Above: travelling by buffalo cart
Below: tropical ferns on the Okinawa islands

KYUSHU

Kyushu's three national parks have beautiful and contrasting scenery. The centre of the island is dominated by the truly spectacular Aso National Park (see page 132), spread around the vast crater of Aso with its smouldering inner volcanoes. You can drive along the Yamanami Highway which links Aso with Yufuin, through panoramic mountain scenery and past Mount Kuju, Kyushu's highest peak at 1,788m. Back roads will take you past timeless mountain villages, terraced paddy fields and thatched farmhouses. To the east, you can hike or drive through the remote, corrugated hills of the Kunisaki peninsula (see page 136), and explore its tiny villages, ancient temples and stone Buddhas. Some of the most glorious landscape in Japan is in the Kirishima range in southern Kyushu (see page 136). You can hike across the chain of volcanic peaks or laze in the outdoor hot springs on the lower slopes.

THE RYUKYU ISLANDS

For those in search of a tropical paradise, the Ryukyus are the place to go. Despite increased tourism, there are still plenty of unspoilt beaches, blue seas, coral reefs and tiny villages of red-tiled houses. Leave the capital Naha and the main island of Okinawa behind you and head for the outer islands: Kumejima with its wonderful beaches; tiny Taketomi, with its picturesque houses and tropical flowers; and Iriomote, Japan's last true wilderness. (See also pages 140-1.)

DIRECTORY

'Here, remember, the people
really eat lotuses; they form a
common article of diet.'
LAFCADIO HEARN
1891

Shopping

*J*apan is the ultimate consumer society and the Japanese are the world's most enthusiastic shoppers. No matter where you come from, you will find more in Japanese shops than you ever could at home – greater choice and variety, better quality (Japanese quality control is legendary) and more advanced technology. The quality of service makes shopping a joy, from the uniformed girl who bows you on to the escalator in a department store to the friendly staff in small local stores.

Set aside time for window shopping. Unfortunately, nothing is really cheap in Japan, but you will find surprising bargains. For instance, don't assume that designer fashion is out of reach: the clothes of such Japanese designers as Issey Miyake and others like Norma Kamali (made in Hong Kong) are cheaper in Japan than in the west.

There is no Sunday closing in Japan; in fact, Japanese shops are busiest on Sundays. Department stores are generally open from 10am to 7pm and close on one day a week, usually Wednesday or Thursday. Other stores may stay open much longer – Tokyo is gradually becoming an open-round-the-clock city.

TAX-FREE SHOPPING
Tax-free shopping is available in department and other large stores, including discount shops selling electronic goods and cameras. Present your receipt and passport at a special desk for an immediate refund.

DEPARTMENT STORES
After a visit to a Japanese department store, London's Harrods, and New York's Bloomingdales and Barneys look distinctly moth-eaten. Their Japanese counterparts are glossy, glitzy, up-market and packed with designer labels. Some are practically small cities, where you can look at an art exhibition, take out a mortgage or play a game of tennis, all under the same roof.

The first place to look for any item is a department store. There are branches of most in every major city. **Mitsukoshi** and **Takashimaya** are the oldest and most prestigious; look there for traditional silks, kimonos and handicrafts. **Seibu** is the most youthful and adventurous, the place for designer labels and avant-garde design. **Isetan** is another store that is good for fashion.

A busy covered market in Naha, Okinawa

WHAT TO BUY
Handicrafts

Japanese handicrafts are of the highest quality and they make wonderful souvenirs and gifts.

Kimonos come in a wide variety of prices and qualities. Some people buy antique kimonos to hang on their walls. You can also buy kimono silk (the Nishijin area in Kyoto is particularly famous for this) and *obi*, the thick brocade cummerbund which wraps the waist. *Yukata*, blue-and-white cotton summer kimonos, are especially popular. Besides scouring stores specifically serving tourists, look for such items in general stores, department stores, even flea markets.

Akihabara's neon lights lure the shoppers

Japanese pottery is made locally in pottery villages including Bizen, Iga, Karatsu and Hagi; Kyoto is the home of *Kiyomizu* ware, while *Kutani* porcelain is produced in the Kanazawa area.

You will also find wonderful dolls; traditional accessories like bamboo combs and hair pins; the most beautiful handmade paper in the world, used to make oiled paper umbrellas, lanterns, fans and kites; traditional lacquerware; and pearls. *Netsuke*, tiny exquisitely carved toggles, have become collectors' items. Woodblock prints (*ukiyo-e*) vary enormously in price; there are bargains to be had in the second-hand bookshop areas of Tokyo and Kyoto.

Electronic goods and cameras

The range of electronic goods and cameras in Japan is huge. You can pick up the latest state-of-the-art model years before it arrives in the west. But don't expect to save any money: prices may turn out to be no lower than at home.

To ensure compatibility, buy only the export model of sophisticated equipment; you can also buy adaptors suitable for each country. Don't buy a computer. The Japanese lag behind the Americans in this area, and your Japanese computer will be incompatible with western systems.

WHERE TO SHOP

Japanese cities are a shopper's paradise.
There are also many regional products
for you to discover as you travel afield.

TOKYO
Antiques and souvenirs
Antique Market
*Hanae Mori Building B1, Omotesando.
Tel: 3406 1021.*
Asakusabashi area
Traditional doll and toy shops.
Bingo-ya
Folk crafts.
*10-6 Wakamatsu-cho, Shinjuku-ku.
Tel: 3202 8778.*
Kyukyodo
Paper, incense, calligraphy brushes.
5-7-4 Ginza. Tel: 3571 4429.
Oriental Bazaar
Every tourist's first stop.
5-9-13 Jingu-mae. Tel: 3400 3933.
Oya Shobo
Two floors of woodblock prints
(*ukiyo-e*), many bargains.
*1-1 Kanda-Jimbocho, Chiyoda-ku.
Tel: 3291 0062.*
Washikobo
Handmade Japanese paper.
1-8-10 Nishi-Azabu. Tel: 3405 1841.

Books
Jena
5-6-1 Ginza. Tel: 3571 2980.
Kinokuniya
3-17-7 Shinjuku. Tel: 3354 0131.
Maruzen
2-3-10 Nihonbashi. Tel: 3272 7211.
Kanda-Jimbocho area
Second-hand books.

Cameras, electronic goods
Akihabara area
Discount stores clustered in main street.
Bring passport for tax-free shopping.

Yodobashi Camera
World's largest camera shop; huge
discounts, tax-free section.
1-11-1 Nishi Shinjuku. Tel: 3346 1010.

Contemporary fashion and design
The Ginza has eight department stores
and many luxury shops. For fashion, go
to **Shibuya**; to **Harajuku** for young
fashion; to **Aoyama** (Omotesando
subway) for the best designer boutiques.
Axis
The best of Japanese design.
5-17-1 Roppongi.
From 1st
Designer boutiques.
5-3-10 Minami-Aoyama. Tel: 3499 6786.

Flea markets
Togo Shrine, Harajuku
1st and 4th Sunday of each month.
Nogi Shrine, Roppongi
2nd Sunday of each month.

KYOTO
In Kyoto's back streets are elegant old
shops selling traditional arts and crafts –
bamboo wares, *Kiyomizu* pottery, fans,
old silk kimonos. **Shinmonzen Street**,
north of Gion, has Japan's greatest
concentration of antique shops.

Flea markets
Kitano-Temmangu Shrine (see
page 82)
25th of every month.
Toji (see page 89)
21st of every month.

OSAKA
Shinsaibashi is the classiest shopping
area. **Nipponbashi Den Den Town**
(Nipponbashi and Nankai Namba
stations) is Osaka's Akihabara, with 300
shops selling duty-free electronic goods.

Entertainment

*T*he Japanese play as hard as they work. There is an enormous variety of entertainment on offer in every city, from traditional Japanese theatre, music and dance to the latest avant-garde performance art or techno-rock. Many western performers – from Michael Jackson down – begin their tours in Japan, where they are guaranteed huge audiences. You can catch American films in Japan months before they appear in Europe. Concerts, theatre and cinema are expensive, but the quality and facilities are the best in the world.

For a more active evening, you can dance (some of) the night away at one of Tokyo's discos or a nightclub or cabaret – but the Japanese night ends early. By midnight, unless you are in a wild disco or private bar, you will probably find yourself on your way home.

INFORMATION

Japan is awash with information. Every major city has several English-language newspapers and magazines providing listings. In Tokyo, the most comprehensive is the monthly *Tokyo Journal*. There are also listings in *Tokyo Time Out* and the daily *Japan Times*, and several free English-language publications such as *Tour Companion* and *Tokyo Weekender*, available from the Tourist Information Centre (TIC) and in hotels.

In central Japan, *Kansai Time Out* and the *Mainichi Daily News* keep you up to date with Kyoto, Osaka and Kobe. The *Kyoto Monthly Guide* and *Kyoto Visitor's Guide*, both available at Kyoto

TIC, are also useful. *Nagoya Eyes* is the best guide to Nagoya. In Kanazawa, look out for *Cosmos*. In Hiroshima, the fortnightly *Link-up* has listings for the area. Fukuoka's lively nightlife is covered by the monthly *Rainbow*, free from Rainbow Plaza in the IMS Building. Look too for *Radar*, Fukuoka's trendy listings paper, published on the 25th of each month. All listings magazines are available from major bookshops selling English books.

CINEMA

Many cinema buffs know Japan primarily through the wonderful films of directors like Akira Kurosawa, Yasujiro Ozu and Juzo Itami. New films by top directors are sometimes given special showings with English subtitles; see listings magazines for details.

CLUBS, DISCOS, LIVE HOUSES

There are surely more nightspots per square kilometre in Japan than anywhere else in the world, from ultra-glamorous to downright funky.

RESERVATIONS
Make reservations through your hotel or at PIA, Saisons or Playguide ticket agencies in main stations and the ground floor or basement of department stores.

Tokyo
Blue Note Tokyo
Tokyo branch of the famous New York jazz club.
5 minutes' walk southeast of Omotesando subway. Tel: 03 3407 5781.

Lexington Queen
Vintage 1980s, haunt of Hollywood stars and foreign models. Welcoming.
5 minutes' walk southeast of Roppongi subway. Tel: 03 3401 1661.

Yellow
Currently Tokyo's hippest venue.
10 minutes' walk southwest of Roppongi subway. Tel: 3479 0690.

Osaka
Oxygen
New and hip.
VIVRE 2B, 2-8-21 Shinsaibashi-suji, Chuo-ku. Tel: 06 211 5163.

Club Jugglin' City
Dance to Osaka's latest boom – reggae.
Komodo Building B1, 1-10-25 Nishi Shinsaibashi, Chuo-ku. Tel 06 252 4201.

Hanshin Blue Note
Osaka branch of Blue Note jazz club.
ax Building B1, 2-3-21 Sonezaki-Shinchi, Kita-ku. Tel: 06 342 7722.

GEISHA DANCING AND TRADITIONAL ARTS

Tokyo
Matsubaya
Dancing and floorshow in the Yoshiwara, the old pleasure quarter, by *oiran*, the top rank of courtesan.
20 minutes' walk north of Asakusa subway. Tel: 03 3874 9401.

Kyoto
Gion Corner
Traditional arts: tea ceremony, flower arrangement, music, theatre, dance. Performances 1 March to 29 November.
Yasaka Hall, Gion. Tel: 075 561 1119.

Miyako odori (Cherry blossom dancing), Gion Kobu-Kaburenjo Theatre
Maiko (trainee geisha) perform traditional dances four times a day throughout April.
Gion Corner. Tel: 075 41 3391.

Osaka
Club Maiko
Entertainment by *maiko*.
V O Building B1, Kitashinchi Hondori, Kita-ku. Tel: 06 344 2913.

KARAOKE BARS
There are karaoke bars on every street – look out for the misleading term 'Snack', often written in English.

MUSIC
Watch listings magazines for concerts by Japan's world-famous composers, both classical (Toru Takemitsu) and contemporary (Ryuichi Sakamoto), and top-notch Japanese orchestras; concerts at the NHK Hall in Shibuya, Tokyo.

Young Japanese are the world's most enthusiastic audience for international contemporary music. Whether your taste runs to reggae, jazz or ethnic music, you will find more concerts by world-class performers here than at home.

NIGHTCLUBS AND HOSTESS BARS
These are largely for well-heeled and well-oiled businessmen; best to investigate on someone else's expense account.

PERFORMANCE ART, CONTEMPORARY THEATRE AND *BUTO* (DANCE)
There is a strong avant-garde movement in Japan and much performance art, contemporary theatre and dance; being generally wordless, these are easy to follow as well as a good way to get under the skin of modern Japan. *Buto*, Japan's very distinctive form of contemporary

Above: Tokyo's splendid Kabuki Theatre

Left: *kabuki*'s stylised dramas are performed by male actors

dance, has received much attention in the west; its major practitioners – Kazuo Ono, Min Tanaka – are legendary names. Another leading figure, Hiroshi Teshigahara, has toured in Europe. Watch listings magazines for performances.

THEATRE
(for descriptions of various types, see pages 156–7)

Tokyo
Kabuki Theatre
Performances twice a day, programme changes monthly.
Higashi Ginza subway. Tel: 03 3541 3131.
National Theatre
Noh, *kabuki* – see listings for current programme.
Akasaka-mitsuke subway.
Tel: 03 3265 7411.

Kyoto
Kanze Kaikan Noh Theatre
Noh performances fourth Sunday of each month except July.
South of Heian Shrine, near Higashiyama Sanjo tram stop. Tel: 075 771 6114.
Kongo Noh Stage
Noh performances fourth Sunday of each month except August.
5 minutes' walk from Shijo subway.
Tel: 075 221 3049.

Osaka area
National Bunraku Theatre
Performances in January, April, June, July, September, November.
At Nipponbashi subway, Central Osaka.
Tel: 06 212 2531.
Takarazuka Grand Theatre
Home of the gloriously kitsch all-women theatre troupe.
In Takarazuka (35 minutes north of Osaka by train), 5 minutes' walk from station.
Tel: 0797 84 0321.

TRADITIONAL THEATRE

In some ways akin to a medieval European mystery play, traditional Japanese theatre is as stylised as opera, with ravishing costumes, exquisite sets and interludes of dance and music. It is, in other words, a glorious spectacle in which language plays only a small part. As in Shakespeare's England, theatre is for entertainment. Don't be surprised if the person in front of you nods off for a while or leaps up to bellow the name of his favourite actor.

Kabuki is the most exciting and accessible Japanese theatre. Its birthplace was 17th-century Tokyo – it was the entertainment of the merchant classes – and the best place to see it is Tokyo's Kabuki Theatre. Many *kabuki* plays portray dramatic events from Japanese history. Villains, in stylised make-up, strike poses; warlords

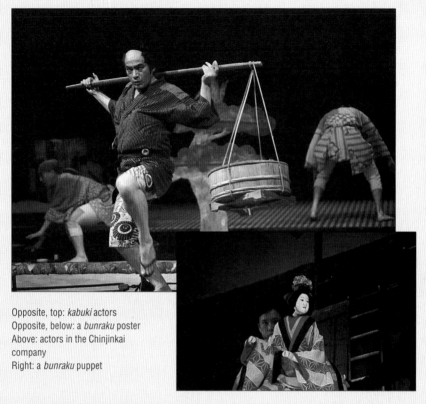

Opposite, top: *kabuki* actors
Opposite, below: a *bunraku* poster
Above: actors in the Chinjinkai
company
Right: a *bunraku* puppet

declaim; samurai commit *harakiri* (ritual suicide) in centre stage. Female roles are played by actors such as Tamasaburo Bando, so graceful that he seems the archetypal woman.

Noh belongs to Kyoto, where there are several schools, each with its own theatre. The *noh* theatre as seen today emerged in the 14th century out of earlier types of dance-drama. *Noh* is performed by actors wearing masks, which are themselves works of art; a skilled *noh* actor can convey profound emotion with the smallest tilt of his head. Few foreigners can appreciate this uncompromisingly Japanese form of drama, immensely slow and ritualised. To lighten the performance, there are comic interludes called *kyogen*.

Bunraku, based in Osaka, is puppet theatre – but don't expect Punch and Judy. The puppets are large, beautifully crafted and amazingly lifelike; capable of the most subtle gestures, they suffer passion, tragedy, love, death.

It is worth reading up the plays beforehand. Translations and synopses of many are available. The *noh* plays, as translated by Arthur Waley, are pure poetry. The *Kabuki Handbook* provides useful synopses of the major *kabuki* plays you are likely to see.

Festivals

*U*ntil you have seen a festival, a *matsuri*, you have not seen Japan. Stripped down to loincloths, erstwhile clerks, businessmen and mechanics run through the streets, shouldering richly decorated palanquins that rest on huge wooden struts. Drums pound out an insistent beat, flutes tootle, dancers weave among the crowds, huge barrels of *sake* are smashed open. When the first Christian missionaries saw a Japanese festival, they despaired of ever making converts.

Festivals happen all year round, though the most exciting are in summer. They are tied to the harvest cycle, and are a way of propitiating and paying homage to the Shinto gods.

JANUARY

31 December–4 January: **Shogatsu** (New Year) is the great festival of the year, when the whole country shuts down. At midnight bells ring out 108 times. People flock to their local shrine to strike the bell and wish for luck. In Tokyo, many people go to Meiji Shrine or Asakusa Kannon Temple. There is a wild Fire Festival at Mount Haguro (one of the three sacred mountains of Dewa) on New Year's Eve.

APRIL

14–15 April: In **Hie Jinja Sanno Matsuri** (Hie Shrine Sanno Festival), 12 floats, flamboyantly carved and decorated, are pulled through the streets of the mountain city of Takayama. Look for the *karakuri* puppets which perform spectacular acrobatics.

Mid- to late April: **Cherry Blossom Viewing**. The cherry blossom appears first in Kyushu, later the further north you are. There's much celebrating and *sake*-drinking under the trees. In Tokyo, go to Ueno Park; in Kyoto, to the gardens of Heian Shrine.

MAY

9–15 May, odd-numbered years: **Kanda Matsuri**, along with its rival, Sanno Matsuri (see June, below), is Tokyo's 'Greatest Beneath Heaven' festival. It involves ox-drawn floats, long processions and drunken revelry.

15 May: **Aoi Matsuri** (Hollyhock Festival) in Kyoto. A procession of 500 people in Heian (10th-century) costume with horses and ox-carts winds from the Imperial Palace along the river to Kamigamo Shrine.

3rd Friday, Saturday, Sunday of May: in **Sanja Matsuri**, downtown Tokyo erupts in celebration around Asakusa Shrine, with more than 100 floats and huge crowds.

JUNE

10–16 June, even-numbered years: **Sanno Matsuri** is more sedate than Tokyo's other festival, Kanda Matsuri (see above). It includes an ox-drawn sacred carriage and mounted samurai.

JULY

14–17 July: the most spectacular festival of all, Kyoto's **Gion Matsuri** originated more than 1,000 years ago as a thanksgiving to celebrate the end of a plague. A procession of 32 floats, gorgeously decorated with dolls, statues, spears and lighted paper lanterns, winds through the city, accompanied by people in costume, dancers, gongs, drums and flutes.

Late July: the spectacular **Sumidagawa Fireworks** in Tokyo.

AUGUST

First half of August: time of the important Buddhist festival of **O-Bon**, when the whole of Japan comes alive with dancing in the streets, wonderful fireworks displays and tending of the ancestors' tombs. It is believed that the spirits of the dead come back to join the festivities. **Daimonji** is a fire festival at the end of O-Bon (16 August) to see off the spirits of the dead. Bonfires in the shape of the character *dai* ('big') are lit on five hills around Kyoto.

1–7 August: festival of **Neputa** at Hirosaki in northern Honshu. Exquisite hand-painted floats illuminated from within depict mythical scenes. In neighbouring Aomori, **Nebuta** sees frenzied dancing in the streets and giant illuminated floats on which warriors battle with mythical monsters (2–7 August).

12–15 August: in **Awa-Odori** there's wild dancing in the streets of Tokushima, near Takamatsu, on Shikoku island.

OCTOBER

7–9 October: **Okunchi Festival** in Nagasaki – Chinese dragon dances, floats and parades, accompanied by the clash of Chinese gongs, all to commemorate ancient links with China.

9–10 October: **Hachiman**

Matsuri is Takayama's winter festival, akin to the April festival (see opposite).

14–15 October: **Mega kenka Matsuri** (Fighting festival). In this wild, exciting festival in Himeji, youths in loincloths, carrying floats, charge each other until one float is smashed.

22 October: **Jidai Matsuri** (Festival of the Ages), Kyoto, in which 2,000 people in ancient costumes parade from the Imperial Palace to Heian Shrine.

A lavish float adds to the atmosphere at Kyoto's Gion Matsuri celebration in July

Children

*W*hen it comes to children, forget about temples and shrines and look to modern hi-tech Japan. There are state-of-the-art game parks, theme parks, amusement parks, aquariums, planetariums, all done with Japanese finesse and attention to detail and using all the resources of Japanese technology, making these some of the best in the world. As the home of computer and hi-tech games, Japan provides a wonderful chance for your children (and you) to try out the latest games years before they arrive in the west.

TOKYO AND SURROUNDINGS

Make your first stop the Ueno area (see page 27), with its zoo, amusement park and many museums – perfect for a rainy day. And check out the useful *Tokyo Museums, A Complete Guide* (Thomas and Ellen Flannigan, Tuttle 1993) for suggestions.

Dinosaur Adventure Park

An exciting river journey through Jurassic Park, with convincingly scary dinosaurs.
Northwest of Tokyo on Seibu Ikebukuro line, change at Tokorozawa for Seibu Kyujo mae station. Tel: 0429 22 1370. Open: daily, 10am–5pm. Admission charge.

Kagaku Gijutsukan (Science Museum)

Four floors of hands-on activity, spaceships to ride in, computers to play with (see page 36).

Kodomo no Oshiro (Children's Castle)

A wonderland for children, with music rooms, video rooms and play areas.
5-53-1 Jingu-mae, Shibuya-ku, 5 minutes' walk from Omotesando subway. Tel: 03 3797 5677. Open: 1–5.30pm (10am–5.30pm on
Sunday); closed Monday. Admission charge.

Koritsu Kagaku Hakubutsukan (National Science Museum)

Traditional science museum – dinosaurs to spaceships (see page 36).

Tokyo Disneyland

The first Disneyland outside the USA is on a Japanese scale, and Mickey Mouse speaks Japanese.
1-1 Maihama, Urayasu-shi, Chiba-ken, train or bus from Tokyo station. General information: tel: 0473 54 0001. Opening days and hours vary with year and season – for details, tel: 03 3366 5600.

Tokyo-to Jido-kan (Tokyo Metropolitan Children's Hall)

Seven floors full of every imaginable display and scientific toy.
7 minutes' walk from Shibuya station east exit. Tel: 03 3409 6361). Open: daily, 9am–5pm. Admission free.

YOKOHAMA

Joypolis (Sega Game Park)

The game park to end all game

Japan is full of assorted wonders and delights to keep children occupied

parks. The pilot shop of Sega, creators of Sonic the Hedgehog, with all the latest hi-tech games – Virtual Reality, Ghost Hunters, Astronomicon, you name it ...

1-14-18 Shin-Yamashita, Chuo-ku; nearest station Ishikawa-cho. Tel: 045 623 1311. Open: daily, 10am–11.15pm. Admission charge.

OSAKA
Expoland

An amusement park in the complex of museums and parks on the site of the 1970 Expo, this has some of the most exciting rides in Japan, including a rollercoaster where you face backwards, a high-speed waterchute and a huge Ferris wheel.

Expo '70 Park, Senri, Suita-shi. Tel: 06 877 0560. Open: 9.30am–5.30pm, closed Wednesday except 20 July to 31 August. Admission charge.

Kaiyukan Aquarium

This vast aquarium in Osaka Port opened in 1990 and features a glass-walled underwater tunnel allowing visitors 'inside' the aquarium.

1-1-10 Kaigan-dori, Chuo-ku; Osaka-ko subway. Tel: 06 576 5500. Open: daily, 10am–8pm. Admission charge.

Panasonic Square

A chance to play with the latest hi-tech from the Matsushita Electric Group.

National Tower Building, 2F, Twin Towers, Osaka Business Park. Tel: 06 949 2122. Open: daily, 10am–6pm. Admission charge.

Sega Galbo

The second of Sega's exciting new game

Guardian pandas watch over the children at Tokyo's popular Ueno Zoo

parks, located in the Port Town development.

O's, 4-5F, ATC, Nanko-kita 2-chome, Suminoe-ku. Tel: 06 615 5363. Open: daily 10am–11pm. Admission charge.

FUKUOKA
Space World

Your chance to experience anti-gravity, go through (abbreviated) astronaut's training, stay in Star Lodge and visit the Space Museum and the Galaxy Theatre.

900-1 Edamitsu, Yawata Higashi-ku, Kitakyushu. Tel: 093 672 3600. Open: daily, 9am–5pm. Admission charge.

Sport

*U*ntil the arrival of the westerners, there were no team sports in Japan. Instead, Japanese athletes developed their skills in one-to-one combat, like sumo wrestling, and the martial arts of judo and *kendo*.

SUMO

No one can fail to spot a sumo wrestler. These gentle giants are usually over 180cm tall, weigh anything up to 240kg and are national heroes. Sumo itself is not a mere sport but Japan's *kokugi* or 'national skill'. It has its origins in religious ritual and some Shinto shrines still hold sacred contests. The sumo ring is marked, like a Shinto shrine, by a thick rope and is purified with salt before a match.

The object of the match is either to push the opponent out of the ring or to topple him so that any part of his body other than the soles of his feet touches the ground. But the final clash is only a small part of the spectacle; the ritual that precedes it is equally important. Sumo wrestlers have a special diet and exercise regime to produce their enormous size. They are superb athletes, astonishingly limber, and much of that weight is solid muscle.

Sumo tournaments last 15 days and start on the second Sunday of the month. They are held at the following venues.

In January, May and September in **Tokyo** at **New Kokugikan**, Ryogoku station. Tel: 03 3622 1100 for tickets.

In March in **Osaka** at **Prefectural Gymnasium**, 2 Shin Kawamachi, Naniwa-ku. Tel: 06 631 0120.

In July in **Nagoya** at **Aichi Prefectural Gymnasium**, 1-1 Ninomaru, Naka-ku. Tel: 052 971 2516.

In November in **Fukuoka** at **International Centre**, 2-2 Chikko Honmachi, Hakata-ku. Tel: 092 272 1111.

Ticket reservations through your hotel or at Playguide ticket agencies.

TRADITIONAL MARTIAL ARTS (*BUDO*)

The martial arts originated as a training for samurai warriors, designed to transform the body, forge the mind and build up fighting spirit. They are similar to Zen, sharpening concentration so that movement and response become intuitive. Many westerners visit Japan to study a martial art.

Aikido

The modern sport of *aikido* – 'the way of harmonious spirit' – was founded in the

Karate practitioners breaking wooden poles over their arms and legs

Victory in a sumo match, as one contestant is forced out of the ring by another

1920s by Morihei Ueshiba (1883–1970). It is a method of non-violent self-defence which involves making use of the opponent's energy in order to make him fall over.

For details, contact the **International Aikido Federation**, 17–18 Wakamatsu-cho, Shinjuku-ku, Tokyo. Tel: 03 3203 9236.

Judo

Judo – 'the way of softness' – is the best-known martial art and a recognised Olympic sport.

All-Japan Judo Federation is based at the Kodokan, 1-16-30 Kasuga, Bunkyo-ku, Tokyo. Tel: 03 3818 4199. You can study judo here or watch from the spectators' gallery.

Karate

Karate – 'empty hand' – is a method of fighting with the hands and feet. It originated in India and reached Japan via China and Okinawa.

World Union of Karate-do Organisations, Sempaku Shinkokai Building 1-15-16 Toranomon, Minato-ku, Tokyo. Tel: 03 3503 6637.

Kendo

Kendo – 'the way of the sword' – is a form of fencing practised with bamboo staves or wooden swords.

All Japan Kendo Federation, Nippon Budokan, Kitanomaru Park, Tokyo. Tel: 03 3211 5804/5.

Kyudo

Kyudo is 'the way of archery', as immortalised in E Herrigel's book *Zen in the Art of Archery* (1953). It uses the long Japanese bow – but the aim is spiritual rather than sporting, being to develop such Zen-like singleness of concentration that the arrow finds its own way to the bullseye.

All Japan Kyudo Federation, Kishi Memorial Hall, Jinnan, 1-1-1 Shibuya-ku, Tokyo. Tel: 03 3467 7949.

Awaiting a baseball match in the Tokyo Dome

Baseball

Baseball hit Japan in 1873. Ever since then young lads have been out on the street, wielding bats and pitching balls. The baseball season is April to October and there are two professional leagues, the Central and the Pacific. At the end of the season, the winners of each league have a seven match play-off for the Japan Series. Tokyo teams dominate both leagues.

The main venue is the home of Japan's best-loved team, the **Yomiuri Giants**: **Tokyo Dome**, 1-3-61 Korakuen, Tokyo. Tel: 03 3811 2111.

The team to watch is the **Daiei Hawks**, whose state-of-the-art stadium opened in 1993: **Fukuoka Dome**, 2-2-2 Jigyohama, Fukuoka. Tel: 092 844 1189.

But the event of the year is the high school baseball tournament in August, when the flower of Japan's youth battle to become future baseball heroes: **Nissei Stadium**, Osaka. Tel: 06 941 5505.

MODERN SPORTS

Until a couple of years ago, baseball was far and away the most popular sport in Japan. Now, with the inauguration of the J League (Japan Soccer League), soccer fever has swept the country. The Japanese are as keen on participating in sports as they are on watching them, and there are ample opportunities for the health-conscious to keep fit.

Golf

Golf used to be the preserve of businessmen but there has been a recent golfing boom. It is still expensive, but there are now more non-membership golf courses. If you just want to practise your swing, watch out for the many multi-storey golf-driving ranges. The **Japan Gray Line** (tel: 03 3433 5745) offers a full-day tour to one of Japan's finest private courses, the **Fuji Ace Golf Club** on the slopes of Mount Fuji (tel: 03 3503 7931).

Keeping fit
The Japanese are in the throes of a health boom. In Tokyo, you can work out at the following:
Metropolitan Gymnasium, 1-17 Sendagaya, Sendagaya station. Tel: 03 5408 6191.
YMCA, 7 Midoshiro-cho, Kanda, Kanda station. Tel: 03 3293 1911.
Clark Hatch Fitness Centre (men only), 2-1-3 Azabudai. Tel: 03 3584 4092.
Sweden Health Centre (women), Sweden Centre, Roppongi. Tel: 03 3404 9739.

Also at one of the cheaper XAX chain; or at many hotels. Check out reciprocal arrangements with your home health club. Outside Tokyo, choices are more limited. All major hotels issue jogging maps.

Skiing and winter sports
A country of mountains, covered in deep snow from November to April, Japan has some of the world's cheapest skiing – though also surely the most crowded. The main resorts are in Honshu and Hokkaido. Japan will be hosting the 1998 Winter Olympics in Nagano in the Japan Alps, and the whole country is gearing up for the great event. For more, see the Japan National Tourist Office's pamphlet *Skiing in Japan*.

This race of islanders excels at watersports

Soccer
The J League kicked off in 1990 and soccer frenzy has gripped Japan ever since. Instead of wielding baseball bats, many Japanese children (and adults) are now kicking footballs. There are 12 teams in the League, of which the strongest are currently the **Nagoya Grampus Eight**, home pitch **Mizuho Park Athletic Stadium**, Nagoya (tel: 052 242 9180) and the **Kawasaki Verdi**, home pitch **Todoroki Ryokuchi-koen Athletic Field**, Kawasaki (tel: 044 946 3030). Football stadiums are springing up all over the country and Japan hopes to host the World Cup in 2002.

For information, contact the **J League**, Sakurai Building 4F, 3-19-8 Uchikanda, Chiyoda-ku, Tokyo. Tel: 03 3257 4871.

Watersports
Japan has innumerable fine beaches and ample watersports. The nearest resort to Tokyo is Kamakura, where the sea is full of windsurfers, water-skiers and jet-skiers. The beaches on the Japan Sea coast are quieter. There are many public pools as well as pools at fitness centres and large hotels.

Food and Drink

*J*apanese food is an adventure in itself. At the top end of the scale it is practically an art form, so beautiful that you can hardly bear to eat it. But there is plenty of good humble hearty fare too.

Be prepared for a whole new palette of flavours as well as a new range of extraordinary ingredients – not just raw fish but wild vegetables, tofu (soya beancurd) in various guises, and even insects.

TYPES OF CUISINE
Sashimi
Sashimi is raw fish – the choicest parts of best-quality fish, freshly cut and dipped into soy sauce with a hint of *wasabi* (Japanese horseradish). This is where the chef often shows his artistry, creating a mouth-watering variety of shapes and colours.

Sukiyaki and *shabu shabu*
Both are made with prime beef, cooked at table. *Sukiyaki* is sautéed with a rich sweet sauce; *shabu shabu* is simmered in broth and served with sauces for dipping.

Sushi
Sushi consists of bite-sized chunks of raw fish on vinegar-flavoured rice. Even if you have eaten it at home, you will be amazed at the range of tastes and

textures: there is an extraordinary variety of fish and shellfish available in Japan, many of which you will never have tried before. Watch out for conveyor-belt *sushi* shops (*kaiten-zushi*), where you help yourself to *sushi* as it glides past and pay by the plate – an economical way to discover which *sushi* you like.

You can eat *sushi* with chopsticks or your fingers. Turn it upside down and dip the fish side into soy sauce.

Tempura
Tempura is seafood and vegetables, deep-fried in a light, crisp batter. The best is freshly made before your eyes. Dip in sauce before eating.

Teppanyaki
A *teppanyaki* restaurant is a Japanese steak house. You sit around a large counter topped with a gleaming steel plate, on which the chef grills prime beef, chicken, seafood and vegetables.

Unagi (eel)
Forget jellied eels! Japanese eel is a succulent delicacy, filleted live, grilled over charcoal and brushed with a rich sweet sauce. It is said to have aphrodisiac and energy-giving properties. Not to be missed.

A humble dish of noodles – the Japanese version of fast food

A classic Japanese meal is a visual delight, as well as a gastronomic treat

JAPANESE HAUTE CUISINE
Kaiseki

Kaiseki is the ultimate Japanese cuisine. It began as a light meal to accompany tea ceremony. The exclusive restaurants where it is served are called *ryotei*, and the service, dishes and appearance of the food are as important as the flavour. A typical *kaiseki* meal consists of many different bite-sized morsels, each a miniature work of art, perfectly shaped and flavoured.

Shojin ryori (temple cooking)

As Buddhists, the Japanese evolved a fine tradition of vegetarian cookery, which is served in temples, especially in Kyoto. The cuisine makes much use of soya bean products – not just tofu but *yuba*, the skin of simmering soya milk and a great delicacy. Watch for *yudofu*, tofu simmered in broth, and *dengaku*, tofu grilled over charcoal and spread with a sweet, thick beancurd jam.

SAKE

Sake is the drink of the gods. There are always rows of *sake* casks in front of Shinto shrines, donated by petitioners. It is a potent rice liquor, made from steamed, fermented rice. In winter you drink it hot, out of tiny cups the size of eggcups, and in summer cold, from small square wooden mugs. *Sake* has no vintage; it is best drunk young, within three months of being bottled or at the longest within the year. Budding *sake* buffs should focus instead on where it comes from. *Sake* from Nada, near Kobe, is 'masculine', clean and vigorous in taste, while Fushimi, near Kyoto, produces a more delicate, 'feminine' *sake*. Etiquette demands that, when drinking *sake*, you fill everyone else's cup but not your own.

A taste of Okinawan cuisine

EATING CHEAPLY

Despite Japan's reputation for outrageous expense, there is plenty of good, cheap food. There are restaurant arcades on the top floors of every department store and many stations, and stations also often have enormous underground arcades, full of restaurants.

On sultry summer evenings, beer gardens on the top of high buildings serve beer and light meals. Most restaurants offer bargain-price set lunches (*teishoku*), and many have plastic models of different dishes in the window, to help you order. Beware of modest-looking back-street restaurants which do not display prices; they may turn out to be unbelievably expensive.

Bento

A *bento* is a meal in a box. These range from a simple packed lunch to a grand meal, beautifully arranged in the compartments of a lacquered container. You can buy *ekiben*, takeaway meals, on stations or in trains.

Okonomiyaki

This is a do-it-yourself pancake/omelette stuffed with seafood and vegetables. You cook it yourself on the table (which has a heated steel surface) and daub it with tasty sauce.

Robata-yaki

In the evenings red lanterns appear here and there along the streets. Where you see one, slide open the door, duck under the rope curtain and you will find noise, smoke, tasty seafood and vegetables, often charcoal-grilled, hot *sake* and camaraderie. *Robata-yaki*, often called *nomiya* (drinking houses) or *akachochin* (red lanterns) are where most Japanese businessmen gather in the evening after work.

Soba and udon (noodles)

The Japanese take this cheap and wholesome food very seriously. Noodles are often hand-made, rolled and cut in the restaurant; they are served hot, in soup, in winter or chilled, with ice cubes, in summer. *Soba* are brown buckwheat noodles, the favourite of Tokyo connoisseurs. *Udon* are fat white wheat noodles, popular in Osaka and the south.

Yakitori (chicken kebabs)

Yakitori is Japanese finger food. Hungry businessmen drop into tiny, smoky stalls, tucked away under the railway arches, where skewerfuls of chicken (including the gizzard, liver and tongue) are grilled over charcoal before being basted with a rich, sweet sauce.

Where to Eat

*J*apanese love eating out. There are literally thousands of restaurants – 80,000 in Tokyo alone, ranging from stand-up noodle shops to some of the world's best and most expensive restaurants – and standards are high.

In the listings below, the following symbols indicate the average cost per person, not including alcohol:

¥ = up to ¥2,000
¥¥ = ¥2,000–¥5,000
¥¥¥ = ¥5,000–¥10,000

There is no tipping in Japan. Hotel restaurants will add tax (6 per cent) and service charge (10 per cent).

TOKYO

(Dialling code 03)

JAPANESE FOOD

Edogin ¥
Legendary *sushi*.
4-5-12 Tsukiji; Tsukiji subway. Tel: 3543 4406.

Genroku zushi ¥
Conveyor belt *sushi*.
5-8-5 Jingu-mae; Omotesando subway. Tel: 3498 3968.

Goemon ¥¥
Amazingly varied tofu cuisine.
1-1-26 Hon-Komagome; Hakusan subway. Tel: 3811 2015.

Hayashi ¥¥
Char-grilled fish, meat and vegetables.
4F Sanno Kaikan Bldg, 2-14-1 Akasaka; Akasaka subway. Tel: 3582 4078.

Kandagawa Honten ¥¥
Wonderful eel in a lovely old house.
2-5-11 Soto Kanda; Kanda Station. Tel: 3251 5031.

Kicho ¥¥¥
Top-quality traditional *kaiseki*.

Branches in Imperial Hotel, Hibiya subway (tel: 3504 1111) and Seiyo Ginza hotel, Ginza subway (tel: 3535 1111).

Matsuya ¥
Hand-made *soba* in a tiny restaurant.
1-13 Kanda Sudacho; Awajicho subway. Tel: 3251 1556.

Nambantei ¥¥
Famous *yakitori* restaurant.
4-5-6 Roppongi. Tel: 3402 0606.

Robata ¥¥
Flavourful country food in an atmospheric setting.
1-3-8 Yurakucho; under the tracks near Imperial Hotel. Tel: 3591 1905.

Shin Hinomoto ¥
Popular drinking hole; fine food, hot *sake*; English proprietor (ask for Andy).
2-4-2 Yurakucho; Yurakucho station, under the tracks. Tel: 3214 8021.

Sushi Sei ¥¥
Ultra-fresh *sushi*, reasonable prices.
3-11-14 Akasaka, Akasaka-mitsuke subway. Tel: 3586 6446.

Takamura ¥¥¥
Kaiseki in a beautiful old teahouse.
3-4-27 Roppongi, Roppongi station. Tel: 3585 6600.

Simple fare in a Tokyo restaurant

TOKYO
NON-JAPANESE FOOD
Southeast Asian food – Thai,
Cambodian, Vietnamese – is cheap and
fashionable. There is also wonderful
European cuisine, magically light to suit
the Japanese palate.

Angkor Wat ¥
Best Cambodian food in Tokyo.
*IF Juken Bldg, 1-38-13 Yoyogi; Yoyogi
station. Tel: 3370 3019.*

Bindi ¥
Indian home cooking.
*Apt Aoyama B1, 7-10-10 Minami
Aoyama; Omotesando subway. Tel: 3409
7114.*

Cay ¥¥
Stylish Thai food and a famous bar.
*Spiral Bldg B1, 5-6-23 Minami Aoyama;
Omotesando subway. Tel: 3498 5790.*

Daini's Table ¥¥¥
Nouvelle Chinese.
*6-3-14 Minami Aoyama; Omotesando
subway. Tel: 3407 0363.*

Il Buttero ¥¥
Fashionable Italian – where the Italian
community dines.
*5-13-3 Hiroo; Hiroo subway. Tel: 3445
9545.*

La Bohème ¥¥
Latest branch of this cheap and cheerful
Italian chain.
*B1 Jubilee Plaza, Jingu-mae; Harajuku
station. Tel: 5467 5888.*

Las Chicas ¥¥
Modern European food, fashionable
setting.
*5-47-6 Jingu-mae; Omotesando subway.
Tel: 3407 6865.*

Siam ¥
Good Thai food, great-value lunchtime
buffet.
*8F, World Town Building, southern corner
of Ginza crossing. Tel: 3572 4101.*

Spago ¥¥¥
Nouvelle Californian cuisine.
5-7-8 Roppongi. Tel: 3423 4025.

Tenmi ¥
Oldest and best natural food restaurant;
vegetarian, macrobiotic.
*1-10-6 Jinnan; Shibuya subway/station.
Tel: 3496 9703.*

Yang Yuen Zhai ¥¥¥
Chinese; Tokyo branch of famous
Beijing restaurant.
*Four Seasons Hotel, Chinzanso, 2-10-8
Sekiguchi; Edogawabashi subway.
Tel: 3943 6958.*

KAMAKURA
There are plenty of restaurants around
the station and towards Hachiman
Shrine.

Dengaku ¥
Charcoal-grilled tofu and vegetables.
*5 minutes' walk north of Kamakura station
along Komachi-dori shopping street.*

NIKKO
Local speciality is *yuba* – soft, sweet
'skin' skimmed from soy milk. Look for
it in the restaurants around the stations.

KYOTO
(Dialling code 075)
JAPANESE FOOD
Gombei ¥
Venerable noodle establishment.
*Kiridoshi, Shijo Gion; in Gion. Tel: 561
3350.*

Kappa Zushi ¥
Cheap tasty *sushi*.
*Pontocho Shijo-agaru, on Pontocho. Tel:
211 7870.*

Minokichi ¥¥
Venerable and accessible *kaiseki*.
*Dobutsuen-mae dori, Sanjo-agaru; opposite
Miyako Hotel. Tel: 771 4185.*

Okutan ¥¥
Simmered tofu in beautiful temple setting; vegetarian.
In Nanzenji. Tel: 771 8709.
Toriyasu ¥¥
Yakitori for connoisseurs.
Shimbashi-agaru, Nawate-dori, in Gion. Tel: 561 7203.
Yamatomi ¥
Great food, DIY *okonomiyaki*, overlooking the river.
Kawaramachi Shijo-agaru, on Pontocho. Tel: 221 3268.
Yagenbori ¥¥
Charming old teahouse in Gion district, full of folk art and ceramics, serving Kyoto cuisine.
Sueyoshi-cho, Kiritoshi-kado, Gion. Tel: 551 3331.

Meet the local foreign community in **Pub Africa**, Kawaramachi, Shijo-agaru (tel: 255 4518).

NARA
There are many restaurants in the covered arcades near Kintetsu Nara station.
Yanagi-chaya ¥¥¥
Nara's classiest *kaiseki* in a 200-year-old teahouse.
Just east of Kofukuji. Tel: 0742 22 7460.

OSAKA
(Dialling code 06)
For wall-to-wall restaurants go to Dotombori in south Osaka or the restaurant malls in Hankyu Grand Building and Shin-umeda City in the north.

JAPANESE FOOD
Agura ¥¥
Classy charcoal-grilled food; speciality horsemeat.
Namba, near Holiday Inn. Tel: 212 1460.

A traditional restaurant in Osaka

Mutekirou ¥¥
Innovative Japanese cuisine, stunning 19th-century environment.
Meiji Yashiki, 2-10-12 Sonezaki, Kita-ku. Tel: 315 8019.
Shabu Zen ¥¥
Elegant *shabu shabu*.
ax Building 10F, 2-3-21 Sonezaki-shinchi, Kita-ku. Tel: 343 0250.

EUROPEAN FOOD
La Bécasse ¥¥¥
One of Osaka's best French restaurants.
Ark Building 1F, 1-1-10 Kita Horie, Nishi-ku. Tel: 543 4165.
Osaka Joe's ¥¥
Serves succulent stone crab.
1M Excellence Bldg 2F, 1-11-20 Sonezaki-Shinchi, Kita-ku. Tel: 05 344 0124.
Ponte Vecchio ¥¥¥
Osaka's best Italian food.
1-1-3 Honmachi, Chuo-ku. Tel: 263 0677.

FUKUOKA
(Dialling code 092)
There is a good selection of restaurants in the IMS Building, Tenjin, and many small restaurants in Nakasu.

Goemon ¥
Magical tofu restaurant.
14-27 Kamikawabata; in Hakata. Tel: 291 0593.
Yoshinaga Unagi ¥
World's best eel.
2-8-27 Nakasu. Tel: 092 271 0700.

TEA CEREMONY

The essence of tea ceremony is very simple. You, the guest, enter a small *tatami*-matted room, where a kettle steams above a charcoal fire. The room is bare, except for a single flower in a vase in the alcove and a scroll with painting or calligraphy hanging above it. Your host greets you with a bow. He puts powdered green tea into a bowl using a tiny bamboo scoop, ladles in a little hot water, whisks it to a foam and, with another bow, hands it to you.

For all its apparent simplicity, it takes years of study to master the tea ceremony. When Zen monks returned to Japan from China in the 12th century, they brought tea with them, which they used as a stimulant to keep them awake during hours of meditation. Then in the 16th century, the tea master Sen no Rikyu laid down the ritual of the Way – the proper way to drink tea.

In the tea ceremony, every detail counts. From left, opposite: seated and kneeling ceremonies; a teahouse; enjoying tea; a teapot and bean cakes

The tea ceremony is at the heart of a whole aesthetic of simplicity and refined poverty. Every implement – ladle, whisk, scoop, kettle – is a work of art; as the guest, you admire and appreciate each. The tea caddy is often a fascinating stoneware kept in a silk pouch. The most central of all is the bowl, often rough and slightly asymmetrical.

As the guest, first eat the small cake your host serves you. When the bowl is passed to you, bow, take it and turn it twice clockwise so that the front is away from you. Sip the tea (the last is a polite slurp). Wipe the bowl where you drank with your fingers and turn it anti-clockwise twice.

There are tearooms in many temples, palaces and castles. One of the oldest is in Nanzenji in Kyoto (see page 83).

Hotels and Accommodation

*T*he Japanese are inveterate travellers around their own country and Japan is well supplied with hotels; new ones spring up each year. Every major city has towering western-style hotels, well up to international standards, and plenty of what are called in Japanese 'business hotels', which offer an economical bed for the night. These are usually clustered around the station. A good way to experience genuine Japanese hospitality is to stay in a traditional inn.

Even in Tokyo, hotels are no more expensive than in any western country and less expensive than in many; in business hotels, a small but immaculately clean room costs between ¥6,000 and ¥10,000. In the countryside a night at a *minshuku* (bed and breakfast) will cost ¥5–6,000, including two meals. No matter how cheap the hotel, you can always be sure that it will be spotlessly clean and comfortable.

At luxury hotels, 10 per cent service charge and 6 per cent tax are routinely added to the bill. Outside large western-style hotels, credit cards are often not accepted. Japan is still basically a cash economy and you should take plenty of it when you travel.

LODGING JAPANESE-STYLE

A traditional inn provides a glimpse of the way the Japanese live and is an experience not to be missed.

You slide open the front door, remove your shoes, put on slippers and are escorted to your own *tatami*-matted room. The room will be sparsely furnished, with a futon mattress, which is spread on the floor at bedtime, and quilts to keep you warm in winter or a towelling blanket in summer. There will be a television, a flask of tea, and a *yukata* (cotton bathrobe). You bath before dinner (not taking a bath is not an option). Be careful to remove slippers before walking on *tatami* and use the special toilet slippers provided; don't forget to soap and rinse yourself outside the bath (see page 19). Dinner is around 6pm and breakfast at 7–8am.

The price of accommodation always includes two Japanese-style meals. Wear your *yukata* for dinner and expect mountain vegetables

Fragrant rice straw *tatami* matting, used in Japanese-style inns

The *minshuku* offers the comforts of home and is readily available all over Japan

and regional specialities.

Local Tourist Information Centres will advise on budget accommodation. The Japan National Tourist Organisation publishes a leaflet on the Economical Japanese Inn Group, an association of *ryokan* (see page 176) geared to foreigners, where English is spoken.

Minshuku (bed, breakfast and evening meal)

A *minshuku* is a family home rather like an English or American bed and breakfast. There are *minshuku* all over Japan, even in the tiniest village. You have your own room, but will be expected to lay out your futon yourself (you will find it inside the cupboard). You use the family bath and will be told when to bath. Dinner will be Japanese-style, served in a communal room where

you sit on a cushion on the floor. For the cost of your lodging some offer a veritable feast, while in others the fare is spartan.

Onsen (spas)

Many Japanese-style inns are in hot spring resorts. Here the main feature is the vast communal baths, divided into men's and women's, always piping hot and full of health-giving minerals. Sometimes there is a variety of baths – a jacuzzi, a whirlpool bath, and baths of different temperatures or different mineral contents. The baths are usually in the basement. Most wonderful of all are the *rotemburo*, where the baths are outdoors and you sit under the stars, soaking in steaming water. Dinner will be lavish and is often in a huge dining room, where there may be entertainment or karaoke to follow.

Turning Japanese in a *ryokan*

Ryokan (traditional inns)

Ryokan are the Japanese equivalent of luxury hotels and offer a unique experience, not to be missed. In the best *ryokan*, the building itself is a beautiful old house and your room may overlook a Japanese garden of stones and moss. There will be a large communal bath, fed with mineral-rich water, but you will also probably have a private bath. Best of all, you will have your own kimono-clad maid, who lays out your futon and serves your meals course by course in your room. The food will be a revelation. Here is your chance to try *kaiseki* (see page 167) in the most perfect of settings.

WESTERN-STYLE HOTELS

Japan has a long tradition of western-style hotels. Some of the oldest – the **Fujiya** in Hakone (1878), the **Kanaya** in Nikko (1873) – are worth visiting in their own right, while Frank Lloyd Wright's **Tokyo Imperial**, now preserved in Meiji-mura (see page 98), famously survived the 1923 earthquake.

Business hotels (economical)

Designed for Japanese businessmen on the move, these provide basic, economical and scrupulously clean accommodation. Most rooms are singles, so small that the bed occupies nearly the entire space. There will be a television (often coin-fed), reading lamp and tiny bath and toilet unit moulded out of plastic: all the necessaries (but nothing to encourage you to stay long) at reasonable prices – from ¥6,000 upwards. Ask at the JNTO for the *Business Hotel Guide*.

Capsule hotels

A capsule hotel is like a beehive, with floor upon floor of coffin-sized capsules, each just big enough to hold a bed, television, radio, reading light and alarm clock. Designed for businessmen too drunk to get home, most are men-only; a few are women-only. Worth trying as an experiment though an experience you probably wouldn't want to repeat.

Love hotels

These are fantasy palaces designed for lovers, whether married or not, in search of privacy from claustrophobic Japanese family life. You can spot them by the outrageous architecture. The weary traveller should note that an overnight stay is very cheap – most people stay only two hours.

Luxury hotels

Luxury hotels are like small cities, with shopping arcades and dozens of restaurants. In the top hotels the rooms are commensurately large and luxurious, but elsewhere may be disappointingly small. Twin rooms start around ¥14,000 and can rise much higher.

Youth hostels

If you want to meet Japan's travelling student population and don't mind a bunk in a dormitory, youth hostels offer a very cheap way to see Japan. Some are not hostels at all, but temples, inns or farms in beautiful locations. There is no age limit. You can often join on the spot, though it is safer to join before you leave home. See *Youth Hostel Handbook*, available from hostels or Japan Youth Hostels Inc (tel: 03 3269 5831); JNTO publishes *Youth Hostels in Japan*.

Thomas Cook Traveller's Tip

Travellers who purchase their travel tickets from a Thomas Cook location are entitled to use the services of any other Thomas Cook location, free of charge, to make hotel reservations (see address on page 186).

BOOKING NUMBERS
Economical Japanese Inn Group
Book through JNTO, TIC or Welcome Inn Reservation Centre – tel: 03 3580 8353.

Business Hotels
Daiichi – tel: 03 3501 5161; Sunroute – tel: 03 3375 3211; Tokyu Inn – tel: 03 3462 0109; Washington – tel: 03 3433 5151.

Luxury Hotels
ANA – tel: 03 3505 1181; Hilton – tel: 03 3344 5111; Hyatt – tel: 03 3288 1234; Imperial - tel: 03 3504 1111; Miyako – tel: 03 3447 3111; New Otani – tel: 03 3265 1111; Nikko – tel: 03 3281 4321; Okura – tel: 03 3582 0111; Prince – tel: 03 3209 8686; Tokyu – tel: 03 3264 4436; Westin – tel: 03 5275 1996; 0120 39 1671.

Youth hostels are often full of character

On Business

*J*apan is the world's second largest industrial economy – only the United States has a larger gross national product – and has achieved an economic miracle unparalleled in the history of the globe. The 1990s have brought challenges, however: a mild recession (which seemed to have passed by mid-decade); a trade war with the United States and pressure on Japan to open its markets; and an ever-strengthening yen.

Japanese companies are fiercely competitive both at home and abroad, and the Japanese invest highly in research and development. But while Japan leads the field in lasers, video, digital electronics and semi-conductors, they are – surprisingly – lagging behind the all-important area of multimedia.

DOING BUSINESS

Business in Japan is as much about building relationships as negotiating contracts: the Japanese like to do business with people they know and trust. The following tips should help.

• Japanese are punctual, punctilious and unfailingly courteous. To do business with them successfully, you need to follow suit.

• Bring a supply of gifts from your company or home country – good wine, Fortnum & Mason's tea, cufflinks, a conservative tie – to smooth your way on first meeting your opposite number. Gifts should be expensive, wrapped in the store bag and carry a brand name.

• Dress conservatively in an impeccably clean suit. Women should avoid heavy make-up or perfume, high heels, short skirts and anything low-cut. It is important to be well groomed: expensive, chic clothes will make the right impression.

• Arrive at the meeting on the dot. Remember that Japanese normally use surnames. It is fine to greet with a handshake.

• Business cards are crucial. Ensure that you have an ample supply, preferably in Japanese and English. The exchange of cards is an important formality – have your card ready to proffer immediately after greeting. Study your opposite number's card with care; never bend it or shove it carelessly into a pocket.

• Never plunge straight into business talk. Your fellow-businessmen are interested not in your company or your product but in you. Chat about the weather, your impressions of Japan, your family, before you get down to business.

• Never turn down an offer of entertainment. Your colleagues will undoubtedly take you out, probably for a meal followed by a hostess bar. This is an opportunity to cement your relationship. Some of the most important decisions are made over a drink or at the golf course.

• Be patient and never show aggression or anger. Above all, nurture your contacts.

ACCOMMODATION

Japanese will assess your status and standing in the company by where you are staying. If you want to impress, there are only three places to stay in Tokyo: the **Imperial**, the **Okura** and the **New Otani**. For more on accommodation, see pages 174–7.

BUSINESS TRANSPORT

Transport is plentiful, efficient and unfailingly punctual – perfect for the businessman. Japanese executives make much use of internal flights.
Limousine services: Drivers Bank Corp (tel: 03 3352 3773) and **Japan Drivers Federation** (tel: 03 3200 4891), both Tokyo, provide limousines, executive vehicles and chauffeurs.

COMMUNICATIONS

Standards of hi-tech communication will undoubtedly be higher than at home.
Courier Services: **Fedex**. Tel: 03 3201 4331); **DHL Japan Inc**. Tel: 03 3454 0501).

CONFERENCE AND EXHIBITION FACILITIES

The major conference centres are:
Nippon Convention Centre, Makuhari, between Tokyo and Narita Airport (tel: 043 296 0001), a convention city; **Pacific Convention Plaza**, Minato Mirai, Yokohama (tel: 045 221 2121); and **Asia and Pacific Trade Centre** (ATC), Suminoe, Osaka (tel: 06 615 5000).

There are other convention and trade centres in every city. For details, consult JETRO, the Japan Chamber of Commerce, or Japan Convention Services Inc (tel: 03 3508 1211). Many conferences and smaller exhibitions are held in the major hotels.

MEDIA

Same-day editions of the *Financial Times* and *International Herald Tribune* are printed in Japan. *The Nikkei* (*Japan Economic Journal*, English edition) is the Japanese equivalent of the *Financial Times*. Relevant magazines include *Tokyo Business Today*, *Japan Foreign Trade Journal* and the *Far Eastern Economic Review*.

A concrete cityscape in Shinjuku

SECRETARIAL/TRANSLATION SERVICES

Most major western-style hotels have a well-equipped business service centre which provides secretarial assistance, translating, interpreting and business consultancy. These services may also be available to non-residents.
Specialist firms include: **Alpha Corporation** (tel: 03 3230 0090); **International Business Centre Inc** (tel: 03 3583 3083); **Manpower Japan** (tel: 03-3562 4271); **Oak Associates** (tel: 03 3760 8451).

For business cards, go to the New Otani Hotel.

FURTHER INFORMATION

Contact **JETRO** (Japan External Trade Organisation), Leconfield House, Curzon Street W1Y 8LQ, UK (tel: 0171 493 7226); 44F McGraw-Hill Bldg, 1221 Avenue of the Americas, New York, NY 10020-1060, USA (tel: 212 997 0400). Or try embassies and chambers of commerce.

Practical Guide

CONTENTS

Arriving
Camping
Climate
Clothing
Crime
Customs Regulations
Disabled Travellers
Electricity
Embassies and Consulates
Emergency Telephone Numbers
Health
Insurance
Language
Lost Property
Maps
Measurements and Sizes

Media
Money Matters
National Holidays
Opening Hours
Organised Tours
Pharmacies
Photography
Places of Worship
Police
Post Offices
Senior Citizens
Student and Youth Travel
Telephones
Time
Tipping
Toilets
Tourist Offices

ARRIVING
Entry formalities
Tourists from most European countries
and the USA are granted an automatic
entry permit for visits of up to 90 days.

By air
There are direct flights to Japan from
most major destinations. The national
carrier is Japan Airlines. A choice
popular with young Japanese travellers is
Virgin Atlantic (to Narita).

Most visitors arrive at **Narita** (New
Tokyo International Airport), recently
expanded, but inconveniently far from
Tokyo. If your main destination is Osaka
or Kyoto, you can fly straight to **Kansai
International Airport**, the futuristic
24-hour airport in Osaka Bay.

To and from Narita: The **limousine
bus** linking the airport with TCAT
(Tokyo City Air Terminal) and selected
hotels is best for those with heavy
luggage. Buy tickets from the Airport
Limousine Bus Information Desk in the
arrivals lobby. Allow up to 2 hours for
the journey. From TCAT take a taxi to
your hotel. On departure, check in your
baggage at TCAT and take the
limousine bus to the airport. **Taxi** from
Narita to Tokyo is prohibitively
expensive.

You can also get into town by **train.**
The Keisei Skyliner departs about every
30 minutes and takes one hour to reach
Ueno station in northeast Tokyo. The
Narita Express is slightly more expensive
(though you can use your JR Pass – see
page 20) and takes one hour to Tokyo
Station. But beware! While seats are
usually available going into Tokyo, the
Express is often booked up months in
advance for the journey out to Narita.

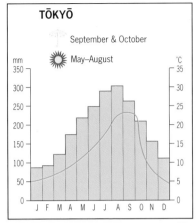

TŌKYŌ

September & October
May–August

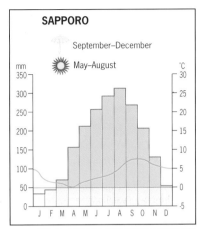

SAPPORO

September–December
May–August

WEATHER CONVERSION CHART
25.4mm = 1 inch
°F = 1.8 × °C + 32

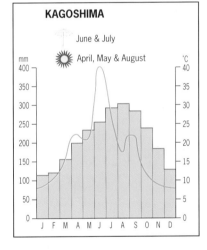

KAGOSHIMA

June & July
April, May & August

To and from Kansai International Airport: Hi-tech **trains** link the airport with the mainland. The Rapit takes 29 minutes to Namba, Osaka's southern terminus. JR's Haruka reaches Shin-Osaka (for the bullet train line and northern Osaka) in 45 minutes, Kyoto in 75 minutes. Trains depart every 30 minutes. There are **limousine buses** to Osaka, Kobe and Nara; you can also take a **ferry** to Osaka and Kobe. On departure, JAL passengers can check in at City Air Terminals in Namba Nankai and Kyoto stations.

Tax: Airport tax is charged at departure.

CAMPING

Camping has begun to boom in Japan. Travellers with tents are welcome in campsites in national parks in Hokkaido, Tohoku and Kyushu. Campsites also often provide bungalow accommodation.

CLIMATE

Spring (March until early May) is warm and dry. June is wet and sultry and mid-July to late August are hot and humid. Autumn is mild and dry, though September brings occasional typhoons. In winter in the north and on the Japan Sea coast there is deep snow. Tokyo is always warmer than the rest of Japan.

CLOTHING

Take clothes that will enable you to sit comfortably and decorously on the floor when required, and comfortable walking shoes which can be easily slipped on and off. In spring and autumn you will need a sweater, in summer the lightest of clothing, in winter an overcoat. In Japan appearance is very important. Most Japanese wear smart, new clothes; you will feel out of place in old or torn clothes. Although there are plenty of shops selling shoes and clothes, it can be difficult for westerners to find items in large enough sizes.

CRIME

Japan has a famously low crime-rate. You can leave your bag unattended and assume it will be there when you get back. There is plenty of organised crime,

run by the notorious *yakuza* crime syndicates, but this does not affect the tourist.

CUSTOMS REGULATIONS

Individual travellers may import duty free: 400 cigarettes, 100 cigars or 500g tobacco; three 760cc bottles of alcoholic drinks; 57ml perfume; and souvenirs to a total value of Y200,000. It is extremely unwise to take illegal drugs into or out of Japan; if you are carrying prescription medicines take a letter from your doctor.

DISABLED TRAVELLERS

Facilities for the disabled are rapidly improving. Many public facilities, including toilets, are equipped to cater for the disabled and wheelchairs are provided at many major sights. Most hotels are equipped to cope with wheelchairs, but railway stations are a nightmare, with many stairs. With advance notice help can be provided at Narita Airport.

Wheelchair hire: Japan Abilities Inc, tel: 03 3460 2341.

DRIVING see page 20.

ELECTRICITY

The standard electric current is 100 volts, at 50 cycles in eastern Japan and 60 cycles in the west of the country. Europeans will need an adaptor.

EMBASSIES AND CONSULATES

All embassies are in Tokyo. For countries other than those listed opposite, check the Yellow Pages telephone directory.
Australia: 2-1-14 Mita, Minato-ku. Tel: 03 5232 4111.

If in doubt, ask a policeman

Canada: 7-3-38 Akasaka, Minato-ku. Tel: 03 3408 2101.
Ireland: 8-7 Sambancho, Chiyoda-ku. Tel: 03 3263 0695.
New Zealand: 20-40 Kamiyama-cho, Shibuya-ku. Tel: 03 3467 2271.
UK: 1 Ichiban-cho, Chiyoda-ku. Tel: 03 3265 5511.
USA: 1-10-5 Akasaka, Minato-ku. Tel: 03 3224 5000.

Narita airport, Tokyo

EMERGENCY TELEPHONE NUMBERS
Police 110
Ambulance/fire 119
Tokyo English Lifeline (Japanese Samaritans) 03 5721 4347.
Thomas Cook Travellers Cheque Loss or Theft 44 1733 318950 (reverse charges)

HEALTH
There is no need to worry about health. Food hygiene is better than in most western countries. Avoid raw fish in the hottest summer months.

Be sure to take out travel insurance to cover health: Japan has all the medical facilities one would expect of such a highly developed and technologically advanced country, but both doctors and dentists are expensive.

Major hotels have lists of English-speaking staff and some have medical clinics. Or call **International Medical Information Centre** (tel: 03 3706 4243) to find your nearest doctor. As a last resort, call your embassy.

INSURANCE
Make sure that you are adequately covered for medical expenses or repatriation in the case of accident or illness. A good policy should also include 3rd party liability, legal assistance, loss of personal possessions (including cash, travellers' cheques and documents) and should have some facility for cancellation and delay in travel arrangements. Travel insurance policies can be purchased through the AA, branches of Thomas Cook and most travel agents.

LANGUAGE see pages 184–5.

LOST PROPERTY
Most Japanese are scrupulous about handing in lost property. If it is not where you left it, try the nearest police box. Public transport and taxis have a lost and found service. Or ring:
Tokyo Central Metropolitan Police Board, Lost and Found office: tel: 03 3814 4151.
JR Lost & Found, Osaka: tel: 06 341 8808.

MAPS
The best maps are free and issued by the JNTO (Japan National Tourist Organisation). For more detail, get the Kodansha Bilingual Atlases of Tokyo and Japan. The Japanese-language Mapple maps are the best for driving.

LANGUAGE

While written Japanese is enormously complicated to read and write, basic spoken Japanese is surprisingly simple. It is not difficult to pick up a few phrases that will make your travels both easier and more fun.

Pronunciation is straightforward, similar to Spanish or Italian. Pronounce each word phonetically, exactly as it is written, and you will be understood. There is no tone system as in Chinese. Give each syllable equal stress. Intonation is fairly flat.

Note that 'ii' is pronounced as the 'ee' in feet.

For information and a friendly welcome, visit the Tourist Information Centre

Titles Always use surname, not first name, plus -san after the name as the equivalent of Mr, Mrs or Ms (never use any title for yourself). Children are -chan. Men and boys call each other -kun. In formal situations you might be addressed as -sama.

Imported words You will be surprised at how many words come from western languages. Often you can simply use an English word with Japanese pronunciation and be understood.

Basic phrases

Good morning	ohayo gozaimasu
Good afternoon	konnichi-wa
Good evening	konban-wa
Good night	oyasumi-nasai
How are you?	o-genki-desu-ka?

Yes, please o-negai-shimasu
No, thank you ii-desu
Please dozo
[*help yourself, go ahead*]
Please give me o kudasai
Yes, just a little hai, sukoshi dake
No, I can't/that's not allowed
ie, dame desu
Thanks domo
Thank you domo arigato
Thank you very much
domo arigato gozaimash'ta
Goodbye ja mata
[*see you again*]
Goodbye sayonara
[*farewell*]
Sorry, excuse me sumimasen
Sorry gomen nasai
Excuse me sumimasen
[*to call waiter, shop staff, etc*]
Excuse me, do you speak English?
sumimasen, Eigo hanashimasu-ka?
I don't understand wakarimasen

Dining
Menu, please menu o kudasai
Just a little, please sukoshi
That's enough mo ii desu
itadakimasu [*before starting a meal*]
Thank you, that was good
gochiso sama desh'ta
[*on finishing a meal*]
This is good oishi desu
[*of food*]
That was good oishikatta desu
[*of food*]
Water, please mizu kudasai
Knife and fork, please naifu to hawk
kudasai
Chopsticks are fine hashi de ii desu

Questions
What is your name? o namae wa?
My name is Smith watashi wa
Smith desu
How much is it? ... ikura desu ka?
Where is the (toilet/hotel/station)?
(toilay/hotel/eki) wa doko desu ka?
Does this train/bus go to ...?
kono kisha/basu wa ... e ikimasu-ka?

Directions
Straight ahead masugu
Right migi
Left hidari
Stop here koko ni tomatte
kudasai

Emergencies
Help! tasukete!
Watch out! abunai!
It hurts! itai!
I feel ill kibun ga yokunai

Imported words
coffee kohi
bread pan
[*Portuguese*]
beer biru
cigarettes tabako
television terebi
hotel hoteru
building biru
apartment apato
platform [*for trains*] homu ('form')
free gift sabisu ('service')
bargain breakfast mawning savisu
('morning service')
England Igirisu
France Furansu

Men's Suits

UK	36	38	40	42	44	46	48
Rest of Europe	46	48	50	52	54	56	58
US	36	38	40	42	44	46	48

Dress Sizes

UK	8	10	12	14	16	18
France	36	38	40	42	44	46
Italy	38	40	42	44	46	48
Rest of Europe	34	36	38	40	42	44
US	6	8	10	12	14	16

Men's Shirts

UK	14	14.5	15	15.5	16	16.5	17
Rest of Europe	36	37	38	39/40	41	42	43
US	14	14.5	15	15.5	16	16.5	17

Men's Shoes

UK	7	7.5	8.5	9.5	10.5	11
Rest of Europe	41	42	43	44	45	46
US	8	8.5	9.5	10.5	11.5	12

Women's Shoes

UK	4.5	5	5.5	6	6.5	7
Rest of Europe	38	38	39	39	40	41
US	6	6.5	7	7.5	8	8.5

Conversion Table

FROM	TO	MULTIPLY BY
Inches	Centimetres	2.54
Feet	Metres	0.3048
Yards	Metres	0.9144
Miles	Kilometres	1.6090
Acres	Hectares	0.4047
Gallons	Litres	4.5460
Ounces	Grams	28.35
Pounds	Grams	453.6
Pounds	Kilograms	0.4536
Tons	Tonnes	1.0160

To convert back, for example from
centimetres to inches, divide by the
number in the third column.

MEASUREMENTS AND SIZES

Japan uses the metric system. There are
various sizing systems, depending on the
origin of the item; in general, the terms
S, M, L, XL are understood and used.
As a foreigner, you are almost certainly
an XL. See Conversion Tables opposite.

MEDIA

There is a wide range of English-
language media, including four national
dailies (see page 179 for business media).
Non-English-speaking foreigners are less
well served. In major cities, foreign-
language newspapers and magazines are
available from specialist bookshops.
Many television programmes are
bilingual if you have the correct receiver.

MONEY MATTERS

Most people carry wads of cash, which
reflects the low crime rate. The currency
is the yen, in denominations of 1, 5, 10,
50, 100 and 500 yen coins, and 1,000,
5,000 and 10,000 yen notes. Buy yen
before you leave home; the exchange rate
is usually better than in Japan.
In the major cities, credit cards can be
used. Visa, Diners Club, MasterCard
and American Express are accepted.

Thomas Cook MasterCard travellers'
cheques can be quickly refunded in the
event of loss or theft (24-hour service –
report loss or theft within 24 hours):
Thomas Cook Group, Advantec
Nihonbashi Bldg, 3-2-13 Nihonbashi-
Honeho, Chuo-ku, Tokyo 103. Tel: 03
3231 2941 can help, or call the UK
(reversing charges) on 1733 318950. The
Thomas Cook office can also provide a
range of travel services for visitors.

Travellers' cheques can be changed at
some (but not all) banks, and in the
major cities only; the process can take up
to 30 minutes. Hotels are faster but offer

a lower rate of exchange. Japanese yen or US dollar cheques are best; sterling cheques are sometimes hard to change. Few establishments will accept cheques in lieu of cash.

NATIONAL HOLIDAYS

1 January (New Year's Day)
15 January (Coming of Age Day)
11 February (National Foundation Day)
21 March (Spring Equinox)
29 April (Green Day)
3 May (Constitution Day)
5 May (Children's Day)
15 September (Respect for the Aged Day)
23 September (Autumn Equinox)
10 October (Health-Sports Day)
3 November(Culture Day)
23 November (Labour Thanksgiving Day)
23 December (Emperor's Birthday)

Banks and public offices close on national holidays. Museums, restaurants, shops and department stores only close on New Year's Day. The week starting 1 January is an unofficial holiday, as is Golden Week, 29 April–5 May.

OPENING HOURS

Banks are open 9am–3pm, Monday to Friday. Most department stores open 10am–7pm and close one day a week (the day differs for each). Other shops generally open daily 10am–8pm; most neighbourhoods have a 24-hour supermarket. For post offices see page 188. Most museums close on Mondays.

ORGANISED TOURS

There are many companies offering regular package tours to major cities and regions. Ask the Japan National Tourist Organisation (JNTO) for details.

PHARMACIES

Japanese pharmacies are well stocked, with many American and European medicines, vitamins and cosmetics. **The American Pharmacy** (tel: 03 3271 4034), **National Azabu Pharmacy** (tel: 03 3442 3181), **Roppongi Pharmacy** (tel: 03 3403 8880) and pharmacies in major hotels specialise in imported western items. There are no 24-hour pharmacies. Hospitals also supply drugs.

Many pharmacies specialise in *kampo* – Chinese herbal medicine; the pharmacist diagnoses and prescribes.

PHOTOGRAPHY

The Japanese are a nation of photographers and most camera supplies are widely available. However, as Japanese prefer prints it is advisable to stock up on slide film in the big cities or at home. Disposable cameras are popular and cheap. You can buy wonderfully advanced cameras in Japan years before they arrive in the west.

PLACES OF WORSHIP

There are Shinto shrines and Buddhist temples everywhere; many are described in this book. There is also a sizeable Christian population and churches of many denominations in every major city. The following churches in Tokyo hold services in English:
Anglican: St Alban's, 3-6-25 Shiba-koen, Minato-ku. Tel: 03 3431 8534.
Baptist: Tokyo Baptist Church, 9-2 Hachiyama-cho, Shibuya-ku. Tel: 03 3461 8425.
Catholic: St Ignatius, 6-5 Kojimachi, Chiyoda-ku. Tel: 03 3263 4584. There is also a **synagogue** – Jewish Community of Japan, 3-8-8 Hiroo, Shibuya-ku (tel: 03 3400 2559). Hindus and Muslims are less well provided for.

POLICE

Japan is a safe and peaceful country partly because it is so well policed. There are police boxes (*koban*) on practically every corner. The police are courteous and friendly, and though their English may be limited they will draw you a map to show you your way. However, if you get on the wrong side of the law you will see another side of the police. If the offence is serious, contact your embassy.

POST OFFICES

Most post offices are open 9am–5pm Monday to Friday, 9am–noon Saturday. Main post offices are open 9am–7pm Monday to Friday, 9am–3pm Saturday. The stamp counter of the Central Post Office opposite Tokyo Station is open 24 hours. Post offices and post boxes are marked by a large red T, which is also used to indicate the postal code in addresses. Only a central post office will be able to handle international parcels.

PUBLIC TRANSPORT

See pages 20–1.

SENIOR CITIZENS

Age is respected in the world's most rapidly-ageing society, and the Japanese are very conscious of the need to make special provisions for senior citizens.
Internal flights: Discounts of 25 per cent are available on JAL, ANA and JAS airlines for over-65s; proof of age, eg passport, is required on purchase.
Rail: The JR Pass, purchasable only outside Japan, is far better value than the discount available for over-65s.

STUDENT AND YOUTH TRAVEL

Discounts of 35 per cent on internal flights are available on JAL, ANA and JAS airlines for under-21s (SKYMATE scheme). To register for the scheme, bring passport, 3x3cm photo and ¥1,000 registration fee to a major airline office.

Japan has an excellent youth hostel network (see page 177).

TELEPHONES

Japan has a very efficient telephone system. Everyone has a telephone and many households have fax machines.

Public telephones

There are public telephones even in the most remote and unlikely places; they are never vandalised and always work. Public telephones are colour coded:

Pink, red and **blue** are for local calls, which cost ¥10 for 3 minutes. Lift the receiver, insert ¥10 and dial.

Yellow and **green** take ¥100 and are useful for long-distance domestic calls.

International calls

Green telephones with a special sign, marked in English and Japanese, are for international calls. Outside Tokyo, it is often difficult to direct dial an international call from your hotel room; except in the top hotels, you will have to go through the hotel switchboard. It is much cheaper to use a green telephone.

To make an international call, dial 001 to route the call through KDD, the official international telecom company. If you are using a home or office telephone, there are other companies which offer cheaper rates: ITJ (dial 0041) and IDC (dial 0061). Public telephones, however, are operated by KDD, so dial 001.

Telephone cards are on sale everywhere and extremely convenient. Or you can use most national charge cards and call direct.

To call the operator in your home country direct in order to make a collect call or a call via your charge card, dial 0039 + country code + 1. For example: UK operator: 0039 441; US operator: 0039 111.

Useful numbers
KDD International Operator: 0051. English Directory Enquiries: 03 3277 1010.
Internal collect calls: 106.
To make a domestic long-distance call and check the charge: 100.

TIME
Japan is 9 hours ahead of Greenwich Mean Time. There is no daylight saving, so the difference is 8 hours in summer.

TIPPING
There is no tipping in Japan – in fact, to offer a tip might be considered an insult. Hotels and some restaurants will automatically add 10 per cent service charge to your bill.

TOILETS
The Japanese word for toilet is *toi-lay*. There are toilets in hotels, restaurants, department stores and stations, usually clearly indicated by a symbol of a man or a woman. They may be western-style or designed for squatting, Japanese-style. If there are several cubicles, there will be a separate queue for each. Cubicle doors may not be locked. Knock on a closed door; an answering knock means that it is occupied. Always carry a supply of tissues: toilet paper is rare and paper towels almost unknown. Outside the cities, you will come across mixed-sex and chemical toilets.

TOURIST OFFICES
The Japan National Tourist Office (JNTO) is there to help you throughout your visit to Japan. Offices both abroad and in Japan have knowledgeable staff, who usually speak several other languages as well as English, and issue excellent maps, leaflets and information on current cultural events. They will help you with travel plans and hotel reservations and are expert at finding economical accommodation.

JNTO Abroad
Australia: Level 33, The Chiffley Tower, 2 Chiffley Square, Sydney, NSW 2000. Tel: 02 232 4522.
UK: 167 Regent Street, London W1R 7FD. Tel: 0171 734 9638.
USA: Suite 2101, Rockefeller Plaza, 630 Fifth Avenue, New York, NY 10111. Tel 212 757 5640.

In Japan
In Japan, the JNTO operates Tourist Information Centres (TICs) in Tokyo, Kyoto, and at Narita and Kansai International Airports. Offices are open 9am–5pm, Monday to Friday.
TIC Tokyo Office: 6-6 Yurakucho, Chiyoda-ku. Tel: 03 3502 1461.
   Besides the TICs, there are Tourist Information offices in every large city, usually in the station.
   Japan Travel Phone, operated by JNTO, provides information and assistance in English, wherever you are, 9am–5pm, Monday to Friday. If you are outside Tokyo and Kyoto, you can call tollfree: for information on eastern Japan 0088 22 2800; for western Japan 0088 22 4800. In Tokyo, tel: 3503 4400; in Kyoto,tel: 371 6949.
There are two other telephone services which provide information and help in English: **Japan Hotline Information Service**, tel: 03 3586 0110; and **Japan Helpline**, tel: 0120 461 997.

ACKNOWLEDGEMENTS

The Automobile Association wishes to thank the following photographers, libraries and associations for their assistance in the preparation of this book.
MARY EVANS PICTURE LIBRARY 10
JAPAN NATIONAL TOURIST ORGANIZATION 47a, 163
KOBE CITY MUSEUM 58/9
THE MANSELL COLLECTION LTD 138, 139a
SPECTRUM COLOUR LIBRARY 4, 5, 31, 32/3, 40, 53a, 53b, 107, 113a, 114a, 149, 151, 167
ZEFA PICTURES cover/spine, 8, 9, 13
All remaining pictures are held in the Association's own library (AA PHOTO LIBRARY) and were taken by **JIM HOLMES** with the exception of pages 19, 32, 35, 37b, 43, 55, 59a, 80, 100/1, 101a, 102a, 105/6, 106, 108/9, 113b, 120, 125, 129, 155a, 157a, 157b, 171, 172a, 176, 177, 182, 183 which were taken by **D CORRANCE**

CONTRIBUTORS

Series adviser: Melissa Shales   **Project editor:** Nia Williams   **Designer:** Design 23
Copy editor: Audrey Horne   **Verifier:** Jenny Fry   **Indexer:** Marie Lorimer   **Proof-reader:** Sheila Hawkins